Coin Collecting

How to Get Started With Coin Collecting

(The Ultimate Easy Beginner's Guide to Learn How to Acknowledge)

Michael Howell

Published By **Regina Loviusher**

Michael Howell

All Rights Reserved

Coin Collecting: How to Get Started With Coin Collecting (The Ultimate Easy Beginner's Guide to Learn How to Acknowledge)

ISBN 978-1-998927-74-6

ISBN 978-1-998927-74-6

No part of this guidebook shall be reproduced in any form without permission in writing from the publisher except in the case of brief quotations embodied in critical articles or reviews.

Legal & Disclaimer

The information contained in this book is not designed to replace or take the place of any form of medicine or professional medical advice. The information in this book has been provided for educational & entertainment purposes only.

The information contained in this book has been compiled from sources deemed reliable, and it is accurate to the best of the Author's knowledge; however, the Author cannot guarantee its accuracy and validity and cannot be held liable for any errors or omissions. Changes are periodically made to this book. You must consult your doctor or get professional medical advice before using any of the suggested remedies, techniques, or information in this book.

Table Of Contents

Chapter 1: Introduction To Coin Collecting

Definition of Numismatics

It is the take a look at and collection of tokens cash, together with certainly one of a type coin-related items, that people have used as currencies in statistics. The word may additionally furthermore be studying cash, and unique techniques of fee humans use for rate of merchandise and offerings, or maybe money owed settlements.

The have a look at includes the physical nature related to the item, specifically its manufacturing year, look, vicinity of manufacture, metallurgy, and the talents of the economic, political, and ancient surrounding as on the production time.

The time period 'numismatics' was gotten from the French word "numismatiques," and the French have been given the term from the Latin word "numismatis." The English time period "numismatics" come to be first used in 1829, and it became borrowed from the adjective "numismatic."

Summarily, Numismatics method manufacturing research and the pattern and way humans used tokens, cash, currencies, and remarkable items in all records.

Numismatics is once in a while recognized because the "king's interest" as it become related to emperors, kings, and one-of-a-kind early rulers.

Money as a Currency

Originally, cash became created to be an uncommon commodity, due to this that humans needed to be hardworking earlier than getting it. Also, it became made with scarce assets, like precious metals, e.G., silver and gold. Using precious stones aided alternate from a selected bodily surroundings to each other due to the fact humans see the metals as a shop of price.

Nevertheless, because of the cumbersome nature of the high-priced metals, it have become hard to preserve the metals to an extended-distance, thereby necessitating the conversion from treasured stones to paper coins that emerge as an awful lot much less-weighted and might be transported snug. Up until now, paper coins continues to be a famous bodily cash form. However, banks and some economic establishments shops silver and gold as a store of fee.

History of Numismatics

The techniques of collecting coins may be traced to the early times of rulers along side Caesar Augustus. Augustus accumulated precise sorts of cash from overseas that he gave out to different remote places rulers to ease alternate contracts.

Petrarch is diagnosed because the first revitalized collector, with affirmation from his letters describing how vine diggers approached him and asked that he buy their cash and understand leaders at the coin ground they were wearing.

De Asse is a brief shape of "De Asse et Partibus," It became the primary write-as an lousy lot as be printed on the coin statistics. It become circulated in 1514 by using Guillaume Bude. Several of the previous coin lenders had been critical individuals who comprised emperors, the Aristocracy, and kings.

Many famous coin creditors delivered King Henry IV of France, Pope Benedict VIII, and Emperor Maximilian of the Holy Roman Empire. It describes why the coin collection exercising changed into termed the "king's interest."

In the 19th century, the coin lenders commenced to prepare themselves in skillful societies that revealed journals to file coins gotten round their terrains. The American Numismatic Society saved a set of greater than 800,000 coins, currencies, and medals, far lower again as 650 BCE, and a library with over one hundred,000 books. Other societies of understanding diagnosed everywhere within the international are as follows:

- The Royal Numismatic People

- The American Numismatic People

- The Canadian Numismatic Association

- The Israel Numismatic People

- The Royal Numismatic People of New Zealand

- The Numismatic Association of Australia

- The Czech Numismatic People

Numismatics in our Modern Societies

Contemporary numismatics is all about producing and the usage of coins, currencies, and medals of the seventeenth

century to alter the relative coin's scarcity they're studying. Researchers are also involved about the levels, errors crafted from mint, mintage figures, and political, social, and economic components of minting the coin.

The current cash observe is now made suitable via present day-day communications gadgets and the internet, thereby making it cooler to inquire about the coin's statistics and percent mind with fellow researchers. Researchers and those obsessed on coins have succeeded in setting up community coin societies and golf equipment to share statistics and information from everywhere in the worldwide, now not neglecting the research substances that the internet has made on coin facts that numismatists can effects are seeking.

Below are the sub-fields for present day numismatics:

Exonumia

Exonumia is how you examine medals, cash, tokens, and remarkable items that appear to be a coin. These objects also can embody wood nickels, prolonged coins, and memento medals. A big class of exonumia specializes in army memorial awards and categorizes the medals and awards by

manner of military institution or occasion they remember.

Notaphily

Notaphily is the way you test paper coins used as a forex. Since the inception of physical overseas money with the aid of way of governments international, the Numismatists had been collecting coins. In the 1970s, reliable international places just like america, Germany, and France got here up with notaphily as a numismatics department to report paper cash statistics in the worldwide locations.

Chapter 2: Methods Used In Making Coins

The strategies for making coins over time have superior. Coins were made in the ancient country of Lydia, which became over 2000 years ago. The approach of minting historical cash became as a substitute easy. A little lump of silver, gold, or copper changed into located on a coin die consistent right into a sturdy ground like a rock. The employees might take some different coin die, location it above it, and strike it with a large hammer.

Medieval mints already made round steel discs and a press screw to fabricate the coins. Though this system became guide, it end up a good buy less difficult and produced a extra dependable characteristic than the vintage minting method.

The United States Mint

Recent cash are minted the use of hydraulic coining presses that spontaneously feed the areas into the gadget. If the device's capability is clearly jogging, it could get charges of over 600 cash according to minute. Such acceleration is vital for a project just like the USA Mint that need to yield billions of coins every one year.

Though this approach is complex due to using automation to yield billions of cash, there are uncommon common processes used by all mints worldwide. The United States Mint is the biggest globally, and emphasis need to be placed on its steps of manufacturing.

The method starts whilst congress authorizes the US Mint to mint coin, then seven artists' gets to artwork to format their idea

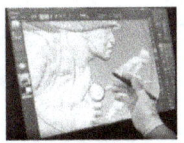

The triumphing layout is therefore transferred into steel, a computer software program converts the layout into a series of

things,

The software sends the data to a tool which carves the layout into a bit of steel developing a hold near hub.

The belief is that the grasp hub is exceptional if we used it to strike a coin, the coin may be terrible or backwards. Instead the system movements the draw close hub to make a die, developing a horrific have an

impact on of the format, the die is used to strike coin.

On the producing facility ground, giant coils of copper and nickels are prepared to be

became cash.

Each coil is set 15,000ft prolonged

The coin gets on rolled thru a blinking press.

The gadget is sort of a cookie cutter, punching small discs known as blanks from the coils.

Next, the collection of device prepares the blanks to be changed into coins.

The conveyer then flow into the clean to every specific protocol manufacturing facility in which they are poured into the pinnacle of the coining manner

No wonder the coin are slides among dies. One for heads and the alternative for tails.

A single strike creates a present day coin, the coining approach can strike approximately 12 coin every seconds with as a minimum 60 hundreds of pressure making one location.

The finished coin then falls proper right into a bin next to each press.

After falling, the operator, then assessments

the notable of the coin

To affirm if there's cracks or imperfections.

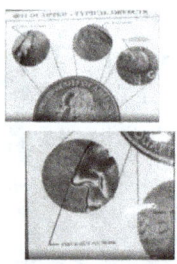

The device for minting is similarly damaged into the following:

1. Mining the Raw Materials

The techniques for minting start with mining the uncooked materials. Mining from in the course of the us international assets silver, gold, copper, and high-quality vital metals. The raw metal from these mines has some impurities that cannot be suitable for coinage.

Additionally, in mining ore to get the important metal, the us Mint furthermore makes use of recycled steel retrieved from precise substances. These materials comprise coins which can be no extra "machinable" and are taken away via move. They are taken decrease returned to the mint to be recycled to shape new coins.

2. Refining, Melting, and Casting

The uncooked metals are touchy to dispose of nearly all impurities. Several coins need a combination of or greater steel types. The metallic subtle is melted, and the brought metals wanted thru the descriptions are included. For example, the United States

Mint makes its 5-cent coin from a aggregate of seventy five percentage copper and 25 percentage nickel.

As rapid because the right pureness of the combination is gotten, the metallic is solid right right into a steel bar. They are large metal bars that encompass the right amount of steel as desired with the resource of the mint. All via the way, the metallic is tested to make sure the important purity is received.

three. Rolling

The rolling method of the metallic bar to the right thickness may be very tasking and time-ingesting. The steel is moved among two tough steel rollers that constantly flow into closer and nearer collectively. This system keeps till the ingot is moved right right into a metal strip that is the precise thickness for the produced coin. Also, the rolling system makes the steel clean and alters the molecule's form, allowing it to be without troubles struck and yield better valued cash.

4. Blanking

The U.S Mint makes use of roll metals about thirteen inches vast and weigh such a variety of thousand kilos. The metallic roll is unwound and compressed to cast off the curving feature from production. After which, it might be taken thru a device that would punch out the discs of metal which is probably now the right wideness and diameter for the coin produced.

five. Riddling

The manufacturing approach utilized in fabricating the metal blanks isn't always clean and is run in a difficult ancient beyond. Little quantities of wasted steel will likely get blended up with the empty coin regions. The riddling device divides the certainly sized blanks from any imported material blended with the coin blanks.

6. Harden and Clean

The mint, consequently, passes the coin spaces within the hardening oven to make smooth the metal to put together for putting. The regions are simply placed via the chemical tub to permit you to dispose of a few thing like dust and oil that can appear at the outer coin element. Any imported material can be inserted into the Coin inside the path of the placing technique, and it's far crucial to scrap it.

7. Upsetting

To protect the stimulated layout at the steel coin areas, all the coin easy is taken through a device having roller devices that get a small bit and train an advanced metal rim on all the coin areas. Such a way moreover enables make certain that the coin easy is the right diameter to strike up in the coining press nicely. After this way, the coin clean is now termed a "Planchet."

eight. Stamping or Striking

At this time, the planchet is now organized, wiped smooth, and softened; they're organized to be concerned. Business cash are fed automatically into the coining press at a level which can get to severa hundred coins in keeping with minute. Proof cash organized for lenders are taken into the coining press the use of the palms and receiving at the least double moves in line with Coin.

9. Distribution

After cash have been taken through the evaluation diploma, they are now organized for pass. Business troubled coins are packed into bulk storing luggage and dispatched to "The Federal Reserve Bank" to be distributed to nearby banks. Collector cash are positioned in precise holders and containers and allotted to coin creditors worldwide.

Chapter 3: Starting Your Coin Collection Journey

What do Hollywood stars Jack Black, Louis XIV of France, and the Roman Emperor Augustus have in commonplace? The answer is that they'll be passionate about coin amassing – and that they have many corporations too.

Continuously, human beings from each walks of lifestyles are interested in this age-

antique pastime. Coin series dates once more to historic Greece even because it changed into Coin collecting dates lower again to ancient Greece whilst it turn out to be accustomed to present human beings with coins as presents on a completely unique event. It is a not unusual interest and people cherished monitoring down uncommon vintage coins or particular memorial variations to feature to their collections. Presently, many humans all through the globe collect coins for the fun of it.

Educational

Coin collecting is not quite plenty looking for

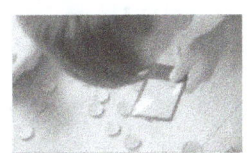

cash and placing them in a field or folder. Coins have plenty records about the time they had been minted and the splendid figures of the time. When you discover an exciting coin, The 'Royal Mint website' is a better supply of statistics if you wish to find out more approximately it.

Exciting

For many human beings, collecting is all about the pleasure of the chase and the achievement even as you in the end end a hard and rapid after months of looking for the final mysterious Coin. To get the amazing out of your hobby, set particular targets for the coins you would like to get maintain of and begin your are looking for journey.

Taking your alternate is a better way of having began out, however you can make bigger your series with memorial cash.

Affordable

Many hobbies need high-priced kit quantities – however, not this one. The collection of coins is outcomes available. Of path, you may spend hundreds at the identical time as trying to find an unusual coin, but for the most critical detail, there are interesting and uncommon coins to be had at an less expensive rate. Even the Roman coins, which might be lots of years antique, may be gotten for modest sums.

You also can select out a particular denomination or challenge, as an example, the 50p piece. There are many exciting designs with no problem in distribution, plus others that can be presented.

Carefully Handle your Coins & Properly Store Them

Although cash are made from steel substances, and we ought to think that steel may be very hard, the Coin's floor might be very subtle and may be with out issue broken. Different metals may one after the opportunity react with the atmosphere they discover themselves in.

When you exercise secured coin handling and garage approach, it allows to hold the Coin's rate from technology to generation. Handle the coins even as carrying a latex glove or cotton. In case the ones are not handy, cope with your Coin via the edge. Most substantially, do not clean the Coin! Coin dealers can inform if a coin is wiped smooth and do not forget it a "damaged coin." This will significantly lessen the Coin's price or in all likelihood make it useless.

It's Not a Race

The way of building a concrete coin series so one can increase in price through the years is not considered a race. Many coin lenders who are in haste to buy come to be being discouraged too fast or perhaps lose their coins whilst promoting their coin collections. Ensure you are taking enough time to find out about a particular coin in advance than shopping it.

Additionally, do not buy the number one coin that comes alongside. Hesitate for some time so you can get the quality of the coin you are on the lookout for for, which also may be supplied at a sincere charge, and you'll be geared up to pay for it. Rightly achieved, coin collecting can be seen as a hobby which could closing for a whole lifestyles.

Websites and Magazines

Since you're analyzing this e book within the inside the meantime, it approach which you need to look for more statistics regarding coin gathering. There are considerable coins gathering magazines like Coin World and Numismatic News. Coin-associated websites also can be a remarkable data supply, but you need to be careful of some net web websites available to sell an overpriced coin.

Join a Recognized Coin Club

A genuine manner to get in addition statistics concerning cash and shield your coin collection interest is to belong to a coin club. Many towns and cities all through the united states have community coin clubs. When you're attempting to find the internet, you may discover the only nearest to you. The American Numismatic Association (ANA) is the most important business organisation dedicated to numismatic training. Likewise, precise vicinity of information coin golf equipment geared closer to errors cash, Liberty Seated type coins, early American copper cash, and masses of others. Irrespective of your location of hobby or information degree, a coin membership may be commensurate along with your goals.

Visit any Coin Exhibition, a Coin Shop, or a Coin Dealer in His Coin Shop.

Although you should buy many cash on-line, unfortunately, you can't hold, have a look at and check out the coin you plan to buy thru this platform. When you visit a close-by coin preserve or a coin display, it will offer you with the opportunity of comparing the firsthand nature of the coin in advance than searching for it. Also, a dependable coin company can offer you the favored statistics to beneficial aid your shopping for method. Several coin shows moreover keep mini-seminars that allow incoming lenders to enhance their coin gathering strategies.

Have a Plan

Before you start a coin collection, carry out a few studies regarding the amount it takes to build up the gathering. If you find out any showstopper coin, it might no longer mean you should now not start the nice collection. You is probably required to attend or keep till you have got enough nonrefundable earnings to purchase the severa costly coins.

Organize a spreadsheet to provide you a listing of the coins you need to finish the exceptional collection. Also, make a listing of the projected charge of each coin and the grade you recollect buying. Check them off your list while you buy a specific coin to keep away from duplicated coin purchases.

Top 10 Coins worth Collecting

Uncommon coins will upload rate and splendor for your coin collection. Pause for a while to don't forget the records you're maintaining to your fingers. It may be likened to a Standing Liberty region carried with the aid of a soldier in the route of World War I. Or likely a Morgan silver greenback that road with a pioneer inside the Rough West. The coin collector need to address those treasures, and any clever collector can also turn them into an investment.

The cash were selected based totally on the imaginative splendor of the coin's outlook, splendor of creditors, and the feasible cost boom over time. You will see an less expensive coin series for the collector that is absolutely starting and difficult, enough for the extra radical collector and truely all people in amongst.

Considering the coin's exceptional recognition, they are regularly the counterfeiter's purpose and "docs for coin." Be careful of buying coins from an Internet coin web website online like Craigslist or eBay. Ensure you purchase your cash from a dependable coin provider and feature them certified through any 1/three-birthday party ranking provider.

1. 1909-S V.D.B. Lincoln Cent

In 1909, america altered the best-cent coin layout from the India Head to a format commemorating the simplest centesimal anniversary of President Abraham Lincoln's birth. The coin come to be right now a success to the overall public. Alternatively, Victor David Brenner placed his three abbreviations at the speak of the penny near the lowest. Former designers use honestly their final abbreviation, and a mint fashion fashion designer referred to as Charles Barber modified the cutting-edge day style. Before the usa Mint facility turn out to be installation in San Francisco made 484,000 new Lincoln pennies, the abbreviations on the again have been taken away. This amendment inside the design led to a proper away shortage.

Although, some may additionally declare that the 1909-S VDB Lincoln Cent is the most not unusual a number of the U.S. Coin.

Many coin creditors began out the journey in their coin-collecting when they picked Lincoln pennies. The 1909-S VDB is the "Holy Grail" of Lincoln pennies with its insufficiency. This uncommon coin is usually the very last coin of Lincoln forex creditors so that it will add up to their coin accumulating. For some time now, this coin has preserved its importance and reputation amongst creditors of the uscash.

2. 1921 Peace Dollar - High Relief

Anthony DeFrancisci made the Peace Silver Dollar, and at the begin, it changed into made in December 1921. The U.S. Mint additionally made an critical mintage of 1921 dated the Morgan silver greenbacks. The notion of commemorating the peace following the "Great War" changed into first encouraged via the use of manner of Farran Zerbe, ex-President of the American Numismatic Association, beginning from 1908 to 1910. The idea become a fulfillment, and then DeFrancisci made an appealing layout symbolic of liberty at the the the the front and peace indicated through the usage of an "American Eagle" at the again.

Although the Peace silver dollar cash were a extremely good assist but have been too hard to strike via nicely, the dies' breaks have been so deep that the metal couldn't float absolutely into those deep breaks and produced insufficient element at the coins. The mint didn't simply start to strike the ones cash up till December 26, 1921. This not on time start gave a splendid insufficient time for america Mint to make these new greenbacks. To a few quantity, they will strike greater than a million coins, and the community rapid took a photograph of them. Though those coins are by means of

hook or by using criminal unusual, a collector simply starting can get a allocated pattern at an cheap price.

three. 1878-Cc Morgan Silver Dollar Uncirculated

In 1878, the U.S. Congress approved the Bland-Allison Act that desired the U.S. Government to buy greater silver portions and convert them into silver dollars. Previously, Engraver George T. Morgan made this format for use on a half greenback. Although, it turn out to be later modified and stepped forward for the silver dollar starting from 1878. The United States Mint have turn out to be fed on through the use of manner of generating silver bucks to meet the Bland-Allison Act necessities.

Although the 1878-CC Morgan silver greenback is not a prime date nor unusual, with about million quantities minted in the Carson City, the Nevada department mint facility, having one of the vintage coins made at the Carson City mint blanketed character to any collection of cash. Distributed portions are moderately priced in the economic plan, which begins offevolved offevolved. Undistributed quantities are as well inside the intermediary collector's rate variety.

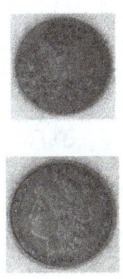

four. 1914-D Lincoln Cent

Even even though it isn't always as uncommon because the 1909-S V.D.B. Lincoln cent, the 1914-D coin is to be had in a close-by close to a mintage of one,193,000 cash made. What necessitates the requirement of this coin is that undistributed specimens were not stored within the comparable amounts that the 1909-S V.D.B. Cash moreover had been. Hence, uncirculated 1914-D styles are more unusual than the extra regularly taking place 1909-S V.D.B. Cash.

Due to the well-known nature of the Lincoln cents and the coin collectors, the coin has sustained its charge over the years, particularly for middle and skillful creditors searching out a extraordinary undistributed coin. Nevertheless, distributed specimens are also in the coin gathering price range of starting and middle coin collectors. Be watchful at the identical time as seeking out a allotted specimen, kind for a properly toned coin without a troubles like dings or scratches.

5. 1955 Doubled Die Obverse Lincoln Cent

The 1955 Doubled Die Lincoln cent is a special coin that is very well-known many of the Lincoln penny creditors. Though that is diagnosed as an mistakes coin, many creditors regardless of the truth that attempting to find to embody certainly one of their coin series. The coin is definitely the most well-known mistakes coin produced by using the U.S. Mint.

The story of this mistake coin commenced when the U.S. Mint used a coin die receiving double manufacturers that were a little counterbalance from each of them. Mint humans observed the error after about 20,000 to 24,000 cash have been freely mixed and available with a batch of effectively produced coins. The mint later discovered that the expenditure changed into no longer properly really worth melting the whole amount of money to scrap the fake coins which have end up jumbled together.

When the replace of this error coin began to seem in nearby papers in the northeastern U.S., many people took out the coins in movement. Local coin stores were shopping them as rapid as human beings must get them. There are numerous undistributed and About Uncirculated examples which may be gotten to your numerous collections.

Regrettably, that is the numerous fakest cash within the market. A lot of those first-rate counterfeits came from China. Be careful of any cash bought on eBay or, for that preserve in mind, any provider that you do now not know. A accurate way of creating an funding in cash is constructing an association with a dependable provider.

6. 1937-D Three-Legged Buffalo Nickel

The 1937-D Three-Legged Buffalo nickel is every different blunders coin famous through the lenders. Owing to the charge and time of production of coin dies, some of the cash have been diffused or floor to unfold the lifespan of the die. A fanatic mint worker overwhelmed the die surface to the quantity wherein it detached the information for Buffalo's the front leg at the back of the coin.

The coin did now not right now get the newsworthiness and admiration of the 1955 Double Die Lincoln cent. As a quit quit result, a bulk of those cash saw a leap ahead. Many middle and cutting-edge

Buffalo Nickels creditors will choose to encompass one in all their numerous collections. Distributed examples are priced moderately, but undistributed examples are unusual, and handiest the coin creditors having a totally deep pocket may be capable of manage to pay for one.

It is, therefore, less difficult for unprincipled coin sellers to take a steady 1937-D Buffalo Nickel and take away the the front leg. Watch out for polishing or scrapes marks wherein the leg turned into as soon as. Obviously, the leg has been taken away; therefore, keep away from purchasing for this coin.

7. 1916-D Mercury Dime

The Mercury dime turned into moreover a amount of the "American Renaissance of American Coinage" in 1916. Although the proper identification for this coin is the "Winged Liberty Head Dime," the famous wondering that the lady having palms on her head end up the Roman god Mercury. Making this coin at the Denver mint in 1916 produced handiest 264,000 coins. Instantly, this led to a scarcity of cash. Adding to the present day format recognition, first-class middle and present day-day collectors may be capable of finding out to shop for any of these cash to embody of their series.

eight. 1917 Standing Liberty Quarter: Type 1

It changed into produced in 1916 with a completely low mintage. Thus, the 1916 Standing Liberty region can be very uncommon and costly. Subsequently, the second manufacturing one year in 1917 is notably sincere in a elegant U.S coin fee sample.

The Type 1 coin traits of Lady Liberty depart her left breast uncovered. Some parents count on that the outrage flashed through way of the people resulted in the production of the second one coin kind by using manner of the usMint overlaying Lady Liberty's chest with a coat of chain mail. A particular principle is that the united statesturned into getting equipped for arrival into World War I in 1917, and the coat of chain mail have become protected to specify that Lady Liberty changed into prepared for battle. Distributed coin examples are reasonably-priced for even a starter collector. A center coin collector can effortlessly get uncirculated samples.

nine. 1932-D Washington Quarter: Key date unusual coin

This coin changed into first made in 1932 and grow to be proposed to be a year memorial coin to have fun the 2 hundredth anniversary of the beginning of George Washington. As a give up end result of the huge disappointment, no Washington quarters were produced made in 1933. Therefore, the state of affairs showed that the layout modified into continuously approved in 1934 and stays in use now.

It has a lesser mintage than the 1932-D, but plenty of them were stored and are preparedly accessible and higher grades.

The 1032-D area is uncommon and will display to be a complicated addition to the collection of your coin and occasionally possibly will upward push in charge greater than the San Francisco problem.

10. 1908 St. Gaudens $20 Gold Coin Arabic Numerals No Motto

The U.S Mint first minted the Saint-Gaudens $20 gold coin in 1907. The first cash had been minted inside the extremely-immoderate harm but then confirmed too complex to strike rightly and did no longer heap carefully for bankers. Engravers on the mint reduced the relaxation in 1908, and the cash have been preparedly made for advent. Many numismatists agreed that the Saint-Gaudens $20 gold coin is the first-class coin ever made by way of the united statesMint.

Firstly, the motto "IN GOD WE TRUST" wasn't introduced within the particular layout with the useful resource of Augustus Saint-Gaudens. The layout emerge as amended on the stop of 1908 to characteristic the motto in the again of the coin. The "No Motto" coin is available at a modest fee because it's far a gold coin to be able to encompass really properly really worth to a coin series.

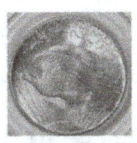

Collecting Gold Coins as an Investment

Before you're making any investment, constantly speak over with an investment guide. But whilst you're organized to invest in gold coins, right here is some proper advice for you earlier than making any funding in gold coins. Recall, in times of economic instability, the gold fee ought to upward push. When there may be a strong and strong financial machine, expenses of gold have a propensity to fall. Try as hundreds as possible not to shop for gold for funding whilst there may be a short boom in rate interior a quick time.

Private Firms vs. Government Mints

The Bradford Exchange and Franklin Mint were privately-owned organizations that put out "collectibles" of numerous kinds and cash. Because the cash created from the personal corporations are not formally from the government entities, many coin lenders were not inquisitive about them. While unique merchandise distributed via using the groups (and their competition) do have severa respectable secondary marketplace well properly really worth, historically, their cash have finished so poorly.

Apart from some gadgets of Franklin Mint's earlier produced cash, sellers vicinity those coins on a length to balance them and pay perhaps ninety% to 90 five% of the silver or gold spot price. Unfortunately, some of the cash produced by manner of way of private companies do now not include any treasured metals. CONVERSELY, the united statesMint is an authorized authorities mint, and its merchandise do almost well on the secondary marketplace, specially over time.

The U.S Mint makes steeply-priced metallic coins for buyers, together with services like Platinum, Silver, and Gold Eagles. The mint gives these cash in resilient and undistributed patterns for coin lenders and highly produced versions for the treasured metallic on investors. These cash have each possibility to be exquisite investments, however anybody you purchase can be subjected in your making an funding or amassing dreams.

Are You a Coin Collector?

If your interest aligns with accumulating fine coins with bullion rate, you will have special funding options. Pure bullion coins encompass the Maple Leafs, Krugerrands, American Eagles, and Pandas. If you are inquisitive about making an investment in treasured steel coins, you have got to shop for conventional U.S. Gold, just like the Liberty twenty-dollar quantities of gold or the Saint-Gaudens Double Eagles. Many exceptional dates of these well-known American cash change at bullion properly truely worth and nearly 8%-10% top price. But, this pinnacle beauty ought to upward thrust at some stage within the length of economic instability wherein the market is active, and the amount of bodily gold is in quick supply.

These coins tended to double their predicted properly well worth: the gold content will usually be properly worth the bullion price, and the bullion is stored up in a one hundred-plus-365 days-antique

American coin. This double detail presents to the opportunity of an increase inside the rate because of its specific nature. We do now not understand the quantity of mint melted inside the course of the melting spree in early 2008 while gold surpassed $1,000 an oz....

Consequently, the ones cash can handiest get scarcer over time, and their expenses reduce because of their capacity and precise nature.

Should I Be an Investor or a Collector?

Firstly, you have to solution a query to understand what you ought to buy, and this could assist making a decision whether or not or not you need to make investments or accumulate. If you're in love with the photographs and designs on cash and you want the sensations you enjoy on the identical time as keeping them and the excitement of concluding gadgets, it manner that you need to gather coins for their beauty and the amusing of the hobby. It can though be offered to profits on a top notch day; many lenders have this purpose in their minds.

Suppose your important purpose is to hold up bullion opposite to the approaching day of reckoning, otherwise you desire that gold will growth in fee and you may sell for an incomes in some unspecified time in the future. In that case, they purchase bullion bars and try and avoid paying the brilliant commissions that collectible bullion cash bring. As in advance seen, you could possibly hyperlink the fence on this thru shopping the equal antique U.S. Gold cash, much like the Saint-Gaudens gold Eagles.

The Bottom Line

Whatsoever you pick out to buy, make sure you take statistics of purchase delivery right away! Do now not allow agencies to store your bullion in their vaults for you! Because if the corporations subsequently move bankrupt or emerge as a sufferer of dishonesty, it way that you'll be held for having a paper observe without any fee sincerely well worth. Take a deliver of your gold and stock it someplace under your law, if possible, at a economic corporation safety deposit subject.

Chapter 4: Methods To Secure Coins

One nicely detail approximately collecting coins is which you mustn't be wealthy to enjoy the severa pleasures that your hobby offers. There are severa

The remarkable difficulty about coin accumulating is that you do no longer ought to be wealthy to revel in the numerous pleasures that our interest gives. There are numerous systems of obtaining coins, which is probably considerably now not high-priced.

One interesting manner to begin amassing coins is to look your everyday pocket alternate. If you do that for a while, you will have hundreds of special dates in all circulating denominations. Finally, you may find out which you have severa replicas. Match the quantities and keep the extra one with a better eye plea. This method to enhance one's series is called "upgrading."

All collectors are looking for for to have the quality viable coin in their series. When you decorate from routine pocket exchange, it's a way to do this with out the high price.

All family individuals and buddies could be inclined and with out trouble be convinced to keep any vintage or unusual cash.

How to Collect Coins

The collection of cash may be a humorous, steady, and pleasurable way of interacting with information and the arena at massive. Though it can be difficult to differentiate common and cheap currencies from unusual, undistributed cash, there are styles to make the system much less tough and plenty much much less uncertain. Knowing wherein to get right cash, what to appearance out for in a buy, and a way to constant your coins will will let you begin a hard and fast easily.

Method 1: Building Your Collection

1. Find a shape of coin to collect: There are hundreds of numerous coin paperwork to be had handy ranging in rarity, length, beginning, denomination, and age. Though it can appear discouraging on the begin, selecting a fashion of the coin to appearance out for will help you awareness and ensure the hunt is going a long way greater great. Recall, there's no specific manner of amassing; therefore, pick out out a coin kind that's expressive to you. Several mind may also embody:

•A penny from each 3 hundred and sixty five days you've been alive.

•One of each coin accessible inside the U.S. On account that World War II.

•One of each usa's lowest-valued coins from the twelve months you have were given been born.

2. Find a exceptional price range for you: Misprinted, Old, uncirculated, and rare cash are cool however very luxurious. Low-price

substitutes encompass in massive aspect disbursed coins, and it could be visible while digging via the pocket trade and bankrolls, or high-quality currencies launched within the present day past, because the U.S. State Quarters line.

A lot of foreign places cash sell for an extended way a good deal much less than their U.S. Opposite numbers. For price range amassing, look for five cent portions from the Netherlands (1913-40), Canada (1922-36), and France (1898-1921) or coins from smaller international locations collectively with Luxembourg.

3. Look out for coins having little placed on: While attempting to find collectibles, virtually open your eyes to have a study out for flat, non-dented coins having some scratches and scuffs. Seek for coins booking quite a few their insightful possessions, connoting that they've now not frequently modified arms. Even notwithstanding the fact that a coin is like 500 years antique,

creditors have to assume for it to be inside the rationally proper condition.

four. Seek for coins that outdoor belongings have tested:

If feasible, purchase coins that have been categorised with exquisite and validity by using manner of agencies which include the American Numismatic Association. For precise coins, make certain they arrive with a validity report from the specific mint.

five Feel unrestricted to alternate: You can start swapping cash with different collectors if you have small coins to your series. You can probably alternate on line on net websites which incorporates Numista, or you could switch with a close-by coin collector within the route of you.

When you switch online, many a time, you may supply and get the cash via the mail.

Method 2: Buying Coins

1. Visit any neighborhood coin hold spherical you: Although coin amassing is a very area of interest interest, maximum towns have at the least one coin hold nearby. Such shops provide many cash at low-cost fee elements, making them a higher region for capability lenders. Many store proprietors are creditors deep down and might beneficial beneficial useful resource in assessing the properly in reality well worth of singular coins, connecting with special dealers, and locating prized, up to date collecting possessions. Some coin shops buy cash right now from clients, whilst others purchase most effective from reliable stores.

It might assist in case you have been expectant that brokers may want to charge up to 20% more than unmarried sellers:

1. Go to coin profits and expos: Although uncommon and not continuously close by, expos, coin auctions, and specific dealings are a higher area for choosing up new coins.

Websites along with AuctionZip can let you find out upcoming auctions, while the American Numismatic Association preserves a list of destiny coin and forex expos on their net web site.

Although eBay and unique principal marketplaces can produce higher effects, it's miles almost tough to test and verify the fee of a coin earlier than you purchase it. Rather, try specialised sites which encompass Heritage Auctions or Great Collections.

2. Belong to a coin membership: In this short period, numismatic organizations can be a better street of meeting fellow creditors, observe approximately drawing near activities, and gaining steerage on how you could broaden your collection and expertise. After a long time, contributors of the club who promote their coins normally provide priority and decrease expenses to pals they've met thru the organization.

Organizations which encompass the American Numismatic Association offer online directories that hyperlink you to shut through and community clubs.

3. Order from a national mint: Most global locations can help you order memorial and strong point coins right far from the national mint. Although mints fee beyond face properly really worth, they commonly add a rate and genuineness of a assured certificates. Mints additionally promote undistributed and resilient cash valued a ways greater than their used contrary numbers.

Method 3: Calculating Market Value

1. Buy the e-book earlier than you buy the coin. A common numismatic pronouncing explains that you need to examine approximately a coin earlier than you spend cash shopping for it.

2. Shun underpriced coins from licensed sellers: When you observe that a deal

appears to be too top to be real, probably it's far. If a coin is undersold, inquire if it's real and hasn't been sensitive to cover mistakes. If you see it at a storage public sale, flea market, or associated industrial enterprise business enterprise, the seller might not recognize the actual in fact worth of their inventory, but location of knowledge creditors and dealers definitely do.

three. Study how cash are graded: Coins are one after the alternative graded relying on the man or woman evaluator or u . S ., however an area really worth of starting is the Authorized A.N.A. Grading System for United States Coins. At this factor, coins are graded on a scale of 0 − 70, with extra elements being furnished to undistributed cash. Letters are included to signify the cost, just like the M.S. For Mint State or V.G. For "Very Good." In the form of machine, the coin with the most fantastic is indexed as MS-70.

Generally, U.S. Evaluators are extra knowledgeable than U.K. Ones. Therefore, you have to be conscious that an exquisite coin in a single u . S . A . Can be seen as faulty in every other.

Several women and men over-grade their cash to provide them as marketplace-friendly. To avoid being swindled, make certain you double-take a look at all of the coins the usage of a favored and licensed "via the ebook."

Do not overlook approximately about that categorizing, even through professional provider, particularly, and the grading requirements can be altered from time to time.

4. Purchase a magnifying glass: Buy each a discounted powered and a immoderate pushed magnifying glass for intense creditors. This will can help you look for small signs and signs and symptoms and barriers of counterfeit, collectively with cash

with incorrect fonts or askew optical elements. Watch out for sparkly coins, as info may additionally have been smoothened away to appearance glossier.

5. Acquire a scale: A reachable digital scale is essential for coin lenders making high priced purchases. Weighing a coin and regarding it to accumulating guides can assist you in spotting counterfeits made from cheaper substances. Furthermore, weighing a coin can allow you to determine its dissolving rate or its in truth nicely worth while melted down into its uncooked materials.

Method 4: Storing and Presenting Your Collection

1. Buy a secure to area your cash: For lenders, who're dedicated, buy water and flame-resistant steady that may be locked to the ground. This will shield your investment from burglars, fires, and floods, a few element in particular critical on the same

time as handling expensive objects. If you're amassing appreciably expensive or unusual cash, improve to a secure-deposit field at a nearby put up place of job or financial group for brought protection.

If you have got landowners insurance to insure your cash, make sure you keep an knowledgeable stock having pictures to affirm first rate.

2. Evade exceptional daylight, temperatures, and humidity: Like most collectibles, you ought to keep your coins in a available, room-temperature environment with little moisture. Avoid basement or loft rooms, places which is probably right away or not right away uncovered to humidity and daylight; meanwhile, all have the possibility of negative your cash.

three. Buy coin flips for separate coins: Coin flips are 2x2 holders typically product of cardboard or vinyl. Comparable to trading or record card sleeves, they hold your coin from the competencies on the same time as allowing you to provide them. Try averting the polyvinyl (PVC) holders because of the fact they may be able to damage the coin through the years, even engraving the coin's ground.

4. Buy coin albums, folders, and forums for whole collections: As the flips, coin album sleeves encompass separate sections effective collectively on binder-sized sheets. They can be presented one after the opposite or with a binder. Coin boards and folders are specialties, cardboard vessels having holes through which cash may be driven into it. These are normally sold with the resource of shape, with numerous folders for quarters, pennies, and the likes.

Chapter 5: How To Catalog Your Coin Collection

Numismatics and coin collecting have a have a examine and gather each coins and paper foreign places coins. It can be a fulfilling interest and a strong funding. Tracking and organizing your coin collection will permit you to hold song of the coins and the manner sound your investment in numismatics is executing. If you certainly inherited a coin collection, you'll be overwhelmed through the assignment you've got got in front of you. However, perseverance and a logical method to cataloging your collection will assist you in ensuring that you get hold of top greenback for the coin series you inherited.

One characteristic that distinguishes "coin creditors" from "coin accumulators" is that they're obligated to installation and catalog their coin collections. To keep a file inside the written shape of a catalog is a vital a part of coin gathering. It does no longer actually offer you with the functionality to look what you presently very own and the potential to chart your potential coin collecting goals so that you get the wished coins to your series. A catalog of your coin collection this is in order and properly-maintained might be top notch now not only in my opinion but on your beneficiaries

inside the future.

Importance of Cataloguing

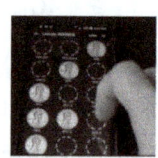

The importance of cataloging yours coin series can't be overemphasized. As a veteran coin collector as soon as said, "We are pleasant stewards of those little works of art work. We could now not take them along aspect us at the same time as we depart this global; therefore, we have to preserve them for drawing close generations." A nicely-cataloged coin collection will permit your beneficiaries to effortlessly liquidate your coin series within the occasion that they do not choice to maintain it for destiny use. On the alternative hand, you can use the catalog of your coin collection to specify which cash will visit which heirs of your own home. This method can keep many headaches and arguments all through the disbursement of your estate.

You ought to enter precisely what's inner your collection, what you paid for, and in all likelihood the well worth in recent times. This enables your benefactors not to get ripped off on the equal time as they want to sell your coin series because of the fact they may understand the price in approximation.

Besides, there are crook effects additionally. The IRS goals statistics to assist the shopping for and promoting information for each of your cash for tax reasons. When you or your benefactors go to sell a coin, if the actual buy value or charge is not documented, the IRS will anticipate that any figure over face fee is the income and vulnerable to be taxed. It is right to document any coin gotten as a gift at the present day market price for tax functions.

Methods for Cataloguing

There are some of various strategies of cataloging your coin series. Some humans might also additionally pick to document their coin collection transactions on 3X5 gambling gambling cards saved in a cigar packet. Others may additionally prefer to use modern day computer software program program interfacing with coin series databases for evaluation. There isn't always all of us right manner of cataloging your collection; you want to choose some thing technique that offers you the critical records you require and one that you may be cushty the usage of. Below, you may locate a few determined on most commonplace strategies humans use in cataloging their coin collections listed:

a. Documentation

A easy three-ring pocket e-book or spiral can effectively help you do the mission for a coin collection that isn't too many. If you've got got a pen and a ruler, you could create columns to enter the specified facts to track. You may be as resourceful as an entire lot as possible and song as an lousy lot records as you require, but the following is a list of the fundamental records that desires to be documented for all coins:

•Country

•Mintmark

•Year

•Variety

•Grade

- Denomination or kind

- Date of purchase

- Quantity (i.E., "50" for a roll of cents)

- Date sold

- Sale charge

- Purchase rate

b. Checklist your Acquisition

An possibility method of cataloging your coin collection on the equal time as you plan on the cash you preference to collect simultaneously near is through the usage of a coin gathering checklist. Unlike a freeform notebook and gives no initial data, checklists are organized through type, denomination, year, and mint mark for every series of United States coins.

Unfortunately, some of those haven't any records had to provide your benefactors or the IRS while it is time to sell your cash. This information ought to be blanketed in your tick list would no longer supply any location of recording this statistics.

c. Spreadsheet

If you very very very own a laptop and a simple spreadsheet utility (like Microsoft Excel), you can hold music of your coin series and every purchase and income information. This have to allow the advantage of together with and deleting lines, sorting your series, and the functionality to right away calculate the charge in the totality of your coin series. Additionally, you could choose out out to music similarly records that distinctive humans may not be interested by monitoring. You can do that by way of certainly collectively with a column for your spreadsheet.

You can make tabs for every certainly considered one in all your coin albums, folders, collections, and so forth. Name every tab in a comparable way in your collection name. This makes it masses lots less difficult for your benefactors to suit up your coin album with the spreadsheet with information on what is inner it. For example, when you have a Dansco Peace Silver Dollar album, you can preference to call your tab "Dansco Peace Silver Dollars."

Within every tab, you may keep monitoring your essential information to pick out and catalog your collection. Such statistics should encompass comparable classifications as listed under:

You can embody running sums at the pinnacle or backside of every column to tune the rate in a total of your series for that sheet. Advisably, located the totals above the columns to let you embody gadgets on your collection below the spreadsheet; you may now not overwrite the general functions in that precise mobile.

d. Software

The fourth and the fine preference is to shop for software program software written for coin collectors. There are severa alternatives for coin cataloging software program software within the marketplace currently. Some are sold for an extremely low amount of cash, a few are expensive, and a few are free of price.

What you're required to look out for in coin cataloging software program application utility is ease-of-ease, the functionality of organizing your collections the manner you want them, downloading modern pricing data, and automatically re-charge your coin collection at the cutting-edge market prices. The maximum modern-day and widespread feature is searching out a well-energetic trial version or coins-lower back safety within the care you aren't pleased alongside facet your buy.

From a few lenders I've spoken to over time, there are three outstanding developers of coin accumulating software program software, and they will be indexed beneath:

v Collector's Assistant thru Carlisle Development

v Exact Change by means of manner of Wild Man Software

v Coin Elite through Trove Software

Suppose you do not know the manner to store, guard, and keep your series. In that case, it may be stolen thru way of thieves or destroyed thru the environment, and a wonderful amount of bucks can reduce the genuinely really worth of your coin collection.

Chapter 6: Tools For Coin Assessment

1. Caliper

Calipers are gadgets utilized in measuring the thickness and diameter of cash precisely inside a fragment of a millimeter. Certainly, having particular measurements can useful useful resource in identifying coins, specifically for extremely tough cash like historical or international coins.

There are considered one of a type calipers, irrespective of the fact that a few are easy to use and function a virtual readout. When you are using them, be very cautious so you wouldn't damage or squeeze the coins.

2. Digital scale

Knowing your coin weight is every other vital size for figuring out a coin. A digital scale is important because of the reality it'd assist you emerge as aware about counterfeit cash, which may additionally look like the actual one but comprised of different slight metals.

Digital scales are without difficulty accessible. Look for a version that measures

precisely to at minimum decimal places.

3. Magnifier

The Magnifier is every different critical device which you'll continuously use to get a better view of the coin trends. A small hand held magnifier amongst 5x and 10x need to be sufficient to have a look at a particular coin carefully. You can take it to coin stores and exhibitions, which includes the use of it in your home.

A vital shape of hand held magnifier referred to as a loupe fold inside its case is frequently used by jewelers. Use any type that you discover maximum on hand for you.

4. USB microscope

An advanced issuer or collector who calls for more magnification than a reachable loupe or Magnifier can get a USB microscope.

They are more less expensive and portable than a normal benchtop microscope. They

are small virtual digital digital camera that is plugged into your laptop thru USB. When you get all of us with a chunk stand or upload a stand to the digital digicam, setup is crucial to get a clean photo. Some have an in-built mild, even though an unbiased mild source may be more useful.

A USB coin microscope is probably essential for folks that want to get into thoughtful ranking, and permit's be sensible; they can also be amusing to play around with.

The fees of some of them are straightforward and can permit you to capture virtual near-up pix of your coins

with interesting element.

5. Task lighting

Lighting should make a big difference on the identical time as grading and assessing coins. For everyday coin creditors, targeted project lights will useful resource coin records viewing. A swing-arm desk lamp is what numerous lenders advocate.

The modern for a gold moderate supply to view cash is a seventy five to 100W top notch bulb; even though, the ones may be difficult to get in America, a comparable LED or halogen bulb is a appropriate opportunity. However, consistency on the equal time as the use of a specific mild supply to assess cash is vital.

Coin Handling Tool

6. Cotton Gloves

Do not manipulate precious or unusual coins collectively at the side of your naked arms! As a end result, the oils from your pores and skin can react with the steel and result in destroying with time.

A lint-unfastened cotton glove is the exquisite desire for creditors because they will be no longer tough, nonreactive, and extra snug. You can use them more than as soon as and, at the same time as critical, wash them. When the coin gloves aren't too pricey, why must you danger your coin?

Even at the equal time as wearing the gloves, keeping your cash through their edges is also beneficial.

7. Coin tweezers or tongs

An greater technique to handle treasured and unusual coins is the use of coin tongs or tweezers. It may be more beneficial on the identical time as extra strength is needed than gloved fingers can provide, which includes trying to find coins near up or for which encompass into holders or albums.

Ensure you purchase tongs or tweezers, specifically for containing cash, as those should have a secured coating thru the suggestions to avoid destroying the coins.

Coin Documentation Tools

eight. Digital digicam

Even the vintage centuries hobby for coin collection is going increasingly virtual!

You'll want to have a virtual record of your precious and uncommon coins, and a number of coin profits are currently on line, thereby causing a virtual digital camera to be a totally appropriate tool. In taking pictures pics of outstanding coins, you'll require an top notch virtual virtual camera with an super macro lens and setting.

9. Coin inventory magazine

Many lenders however want to have a written report of their coin collection. If you visit coin exhibitions or stores, you need to realise what you've got already were given and what you need. Keep the tough replica of your series inventory up to date because of the reality the technique can be amusing in a digital worldwide, even though it's moreover first-class to hold a digital or spreadsheet reproduction.

Journals on inventory could be extra explanatory for the small hobbyist collection and are perfect for starters.

Tools for storing coin

10. Coin folder

At this aspect, let us take a look at options for coin garage from the lowest to more shielding. Coin folders are the stressless manner for long-term coin storing and are pinnacle for beginners and children.

They appear as a book cover having inset circles at the inner ground for containing a coin. They may be popped into the card to be saved in vicinity; the folders can then be stored popularity on a bookshelf.

Ensure you purchase coin folders crafted from appropriate archival materials (acid-free and pH independent) for the purpose that steady paper, cardboard, and glue can harm cash with time.

11. Coin tubes

Coin tubes are tubes created out of plastic that money can be saved in. They are associated with the paper tubes applied in banks; tubes save hundreds of coins organized in vertical stacks. They are an green opportunity for saving large coins but are absolutely shielding, so they are not first rate in your maximum valuable or uncommon cash.

12. Coin albums

Coin album is like photo albums however for cash! They use a binder tool with a plastic web page that has an entire lot of sleeves for placing cash.

They will usually be set first in 2 through 2 inches cardboard holders (named 2 x 2s), then slid proper right into a plastic pocket at the album internet web page. Thus, the garage gadget is related to folders however consists of safeguarding plastic shielding the coins.

You can go through albums to without difficulty check each facets of the coins, and

that they can be taken from the pages with out tons pressure.

Always purchase archival super non-PVC pages and albums so discharges from the plastic will now not wreck the coins.

13. Coin pills

The coin pills are also recognized as coin holders, and they may be small plastic times which are transparently meant to cope with a single coin. Apart from coin blocks which may be sealed and continuously sealed through specialists, those tablets deliver few of the best protection.

Coin holders or pills are bought thru duration for a selected coin.

Coin pills or holders are bought thru length for unique cash. Though now not strictly airtight, they may be capable of offer higher protection from the additives. They are a concrete DIY selection in your valued coins.

14. Flat-clinch stapler

You can be questioning why a stapler could be indexed amongst the ones equipment at the same time as using 2 X 2s; the card approximately the coin should be stapled to keep it secured and tight. A authentic stapler can dispense extended factors that might hitch on plastic albums pages or break close-by way of the usage of manner of cash.

A flat-clinch stapler makes metal staples flatter to the web page; that is a applicable

opinion for the collection.

15. Dehumidifier

Serious collectors must apprehend that water is a rival of coins! The thriller of getting properly prolonged-term coin garage is to keep them dry and cool. To regular your precious cash from oxidizing, encompass a desiccant packet in your subject for storage or spend money on an electric dehumidifier.

Desiccant packets that eat moisture from the air want to be substituted through the years, at the same time as a small digital dehumidifier is a further organized long-time period choice.

Chapter 7: Coin Grading

The essential purpose to grade your coin is thru figuring out the coin's market definitely well really worth. Determining the actually truely worth of a coin relies upon on how nicely the coin grow to be to begin with struck, the volume of the coin's protection, and what form of harm and placed on the coin has sustained. For masses beneficial motive, specially for novices, we're capable of consciousness on assessing the quantity of clothing the coin has and in which it suits at the 70-element scale.

Recall that coin grading isn't always precisely generation; it's miles a view based on a preferred definition that many numismatists and coin dealers would in all likelihood approve. The disparity ground while little data in a coin's appearance also can push it to an top grade if it's an exquisite effect. In evaluation, the dissimilarity is probably a small illness pushed right into a decrease grade. The function and size of the challenge and its final outcomes on the advent are in which a person may additionally moreover grade the coin better, and each other can grade the coin decrease.

Examine the coins which have been successfully graded via reliable coin sellers and check why they may be being graded that way. If you are unsure why a specific coin has a sure grading, ask the coin dealer to provide an reason behind it higher. Coin dealers are continually prepared to percentage what they recognize and make a properly-knowledgeable coin collector. Alternatively, search for a valued and dependable coin company amongst professional coin collectors. Some of these coin dealers normally have a tendency to over-grade their cash to sell them better. If you move and sell that coin, relied on coin sellers nicely grade the coin, and you received't be capable of get your money decrease lower back; you initially overpaid for the coin.

1. The 70-Point Coin Grading Scale

If the numismatists grade cash, they'll accept a numeric charge on the Sheldon Scale. The Sheldon Scale varies from Poor (P-1) to Perfect Mint State (MS-70). At first, cash had been graded with adjectives to outline the coin scenario (Fair, Good, Excellent, Etc.). Awkwardly, coin creditors and coin sellers had opposing motives to the this means that of each of these terms.

In the Seventies, numismatists professionals have been given together and agreed-upon coin grading standards. These numismatists now allocate grades at critical points and the primary goal grade. The most not unusual coin grades are as follows:

•(P-1) Poor - Hardly recognizable and possibly broken; there need to be a date and mintmark used, if not pretty thrashed.

•(FR-2) Fair – Almost worn clean however lacks the harmful a coin graded "Poor" commonly has. Sufficient records need to hold to classify the coin

•(G-four) Good - Deeply worn to the quantity that engravings be a part of the rims in locations; important tendencies are generally destroyed.

•(VG-8) Very Good- Very worn, however every important layout element is plain, even though faint. Maybe if any important element remains.

•(F-12) Fine – It's masses worn, but placed on is even, and the overall format factors are outstandingly ambitious. Nearly completely-indifferent rims from the area.

•(VF-20) It's very Fine – Averagely worn, having a few progressed information persisting. Every LIBERTY letters or the mottos are smooth. The edges on each facets of the coin are entire and indifferent from the arena.

•(EF-forty) It's rather Fine − despite the fact that gently worn; every tool is apparent, important gadgets are clearer. The finer feature is obvious and formidable however may also advise slight wear.

•(AU-50) It's about Undistributed - Slight guidelines of harm on great factors of the coin's layout; there can be a contact mark, and the manner it seems to the eyes have to be suitable.

•(AU-fifty eight) It's very preference approximately undistributed - Smallest signs of wear and tear marks, no essential contact marks, nearly full mint polish, and first rate eye appeal.

•(MS-60) Mint country Basal - Severely undistributed; no indication of damage and tear on the most points of the coin but a terrible coin having clean contact marks, subdued luster, hairlines, and so forth.

•(MS-63) Mint state Acceptable − Undistributed, but having nicks and speak to marks, to some extent impaired luster, essentially appealing look. The strike is average to susceptible.

•(MS-sixty 5) Mint State Selection — Undistributed having solid mint luster, very unsatisfactory contact marks, awesome eye attraction. The strike is beyond common.

•(MS-68) Mint State Premium Quality — Undistributed having impeccable luster, no visible touch marks to the uncovered eye, extraordinary eye appeal. The strike is stunning and sharp.

•(MS-69) Mint State Nearly Perfect — Undistributed having tremendous luster, stunning and sharp strike, and really tremendous eye attraction. An notable coin apart from having a few little flaws (can exceptional be extremely good under 8x magnification) in a strike, planchet, or contact marks.

•(MS-70) Mint State Perfect - The particular coin. While the usage of a microscope, vital beneath the 8x intensification has a pointy strike, and the coin is distinguishably focused on an splendid planchet. Full and bright, precise luster and excellent eye enchantment that is hardly ever discovered on a coin.

The Three Coin-Grading Buckets

The coin grading component this is generally misinterpreted from the novice's view is how the grading scale skills. Consider it as taking three "buckets."

The first bucket is for disbursed cash, the second one bucket is about undistributed (AU) cash, and the zero.33 is for Undistributed (Mint State, or MS) cash.

Distributed cash have the most essential grading scale. It ranges from P-1 to EF-forty 9 grades. P-run, or horrible, is the least grade a coin may be graded. This coin is identified even though it has heavy located on and almost all elements had been wiped out. At the better a part of the size, this could be a distributed coin with slight put on on the most elements of the coin and preserve it from the About Uncirculated category.

Also, the AU scale element begins at 50 and runs through fifty nine. The AU-50 coin can also never have commercially circulated, however because of its scuff marks attachment, it's been via numerous coin-counting machines and given a small amount; it's far no extra in Mint State. Therefore, they're stored in the AU bucket and given the bottom grade of AU-50 if it's miles unsightly and AU-fifty eight if now not. Although this is overgeneralizing a chunk, notwithstanding the fact that, it clarifies the motive the grading scale has to transport from "attractive cash" to "ugly cash" and then decrease again to "attractive."

The MS scale (from MS-60 to MS-70) isn't always actually to hold the previous scale of AU coins, a separated mini-scale of eleven grades that starts offevolved with the dominion of basal (MS-60 undistributed coin). This is an ugly, no-luster dog, bag-marked, strictly undistributed. By evaluation, the AU-fifty 8 coin below it has a beautiful attraction of the eyes and almost entire luster. The reason of a coin grading an AU-fifty eight is that it seems more attractive than a coin grading MS-60. Furthermore, they may be in one in every of a kind "buckets" of the grading scale.

Grading Circulated Coins

The 1/3 bucket is the form of circulated grades, from P-1 to EF-40 nine (notwithstanding the fact that EF-45 is the higher circulated grade you may likely see being used). A lot of starters searching out for grading possibilities have circulated coins, and fortunately, circulated cash are much less complicated for the novice to grade, letting them have a Mint State (i.E., uncirculated) sample of the coin class beneath scenario to make critiques to, no matter the fact that, this isn't a situation.

Step 1: To start with, you'll require an first-rate slight deliver, much like the one hundred-watt bulb in a lamp near wherein you are sitting. Also, if possible, you can require a decent magnifier, a few issue magnifying about five to 8 times (expressed as 5x to 8x). Anything sturdier than 8x is not commonly used coin grading coin, and some factor lesser than 5x is truly too feeble to view critical info and little marks of damage.

Step 2: Decide the "bucket" your coin ought to fit in. Is it Uncirculated (Mint State)? Does it have in reality the slightest clues of damage on the pinnacle elements (About Uncirculated)? Or does it belong to the very commonplace bucket, the Circulated coin bucket?

Step three: You can suit your coin to the scale displayed on the top to apprehend in which it fits on the dimensions. Bearing in thoughts that figures are not related, the quantity of detail out of region among EF-20 and EF-forty is not much like those missing amongst EF-forty and MS-60 (consider that they may be separate buckets.) The coin grading EF-40 has misplaced pretty tons five% to 10% of its feature, but the coin grading F-20 has out of region nearly 60%. Use the inscribed snap shots to place your coin inside the fine feasible manner. If you need greater correct grading, use "The Certified ANA Grading Standards" ebook that breaks the grades out for every number one U.S. Coin elegance, at the facet of photographs to permit you to determine the proper grade.

Since you presently apprehend the strategies of coin grading, you could now compare the charge of your coin.

Chapter 8: Selling Your Coin And Working With Coin Dealers

There is a small doubt that, besides the U.S. Mint, coin sellers are maybe the most normally criticized game enthusiasts inside the coin organisation. Many lenders bear in mind that sellers are not crucial for the internet age and others query their values.

The Coin Dealer Newsletter presently posted an exciting article on whether or not or not or no longer coin dealers even want to exist. The smooth solution is that in the event that they did no longer exist, they could have to be created.

Better sellers generally growth close to own family individuals with their clients and communicate records about coins and the market that lenders can't get somewhere else. In this form of state of affairs, you are gaining from their wealth of studies.

We have every so often heard stories regarding dealers who paid pennies on the greenback to someone having well knowledgeable about what they have been selling. Besides, that is excellent to the rule. Besides, one is simply required to pick out a coin provider, whether or not or now not buying or promoting, carefully.

I truly have had my percentage of awful reports, specifically with mail-order corporations that normally sell over graded cash. This is a analyzing machine all people has to go through. One generally hears horrible comments from lenders selling their coins to sellers, who've been disillusioned with the quantity they obtained and grew to become off through the revel in. A better manner to avoid this experience is to be armed with know-how.

Learn the whole lot you may about your coins, have a take a look at the marketplace, try finding out what the wholesale purchase and promote charges are for your devices, and understand tons approximately a dealer before you promote to them.

Check how prolonged they had been within the corporation and the expert agencies. Being an ANA member is likewise useful and way that they accept as actual with the ANA's code of behavior.

Binding arbitration can be asked via the ANA in case you experience you've got been created by using the use of a dealer who is additionally a member. There are numerous interesting reminiscences approximately this in previous problems of The Numismatist, the ANA's month-to-month mag.

Dealers who're PNG participants, the Professional Numismatists Guild (PNG), are held to better requirements of morals. If you're choosing a dealer to shop for from or promote to, I will now not shrink back from the precept game enthusiasts which consist of Legend or Stack's simply due to the reality you are a respectable collector.

Such agencies do emphasize extra on the higher marketplace prevent and characteristic severa wealthy clients. Still, masses of them furthermore sell items at an intensive shape of price elements and offer the extra notable collector a higher carrier than you could do not forget.

The blessings of dealing with them are numerous, from having higher awesome coins that can possibly outdo decrease-tremendous samples to the protection that you realize your quantities are proper, or as a minimum high satisfactory to be. Selling your coin may be a difficult mission, and that is why you ought to not rush into doing so.

Firstly, one needs to decide the course to take: public sale employer or retail it your self thru e-Bay, at a coin exhibition, or some other platform for selling.

When you have got a higher grade and notable or unusual gadgets, in all likelihood, an auction is the way to transport, but maintain in thoughts that you'll pay a tremendous supplier's fee in maximum instances.

Many people currently traded their coins through e-Bay. That might be a better platform depending on different factors, however earlier than you pick out that as in competition to promoting to a supplier, I have to propose you do some calculations.

Elements in promoting costs, list prices, which may be typically 9%, insertion expenses in some times, and the shipping rate and insure your item, which may be large for pricey cash.

Also, there may be the time it takes to make a awesome list and why you must wait to discover if the item sells. You are nonetheless out of the insertion and list fees if it would not. This leaves the selection many humans decide out for, promoting to a issuer – each your community provider, at a coin exhibition, or via the mail if you cope with the number one issuer who buys just like the APMEX. If you carefully pick out out a dependable provider with many reports, you may most in all likelihood get it at an low value price.

The purchase-promote margins range quite a chunk, even though it is predicated upon at the form of coin you want to sell. If you have got a few factor that is liable to take time for the provider to promote and has many, you will get keep of some thing smaller. You can also additionally desire to attempt a person else specializing in that shape of coin, which can be able to pay greater.

If you promote a favored valuable metal coin having a difficult wholesale marketplace, similar to the PCGS and NGC graded everyday pre-1933 gold, or higher contemporary-day U.S. Mint merchandise having low mintages, maybe in all likelihood, you may get a fee this is at minimal equal to what you may acquire while you retail the coin thru an internet.

Dealers buy and sells such coin on very decreased margins in massive and make their cash in quantity; in the intervening time, there needs to be a larger income on lower-end devices for repayment for the extra time it takes to promote them. Remember that on the same time as advertising and advertising such an item in masses of conditions, you're advertising to a dealer who can in all likelihood wholesale the coin to a terrific company for a little income instead of seeking to promote it of their shop or on their internet net web page.

One moreover has to don't forget that dealers have many costs from coverage for hire, taxes, personnel costs, and so on. While making geared up to promote all your collections or an high-quality amount of the cash, I ought to recommend that you do no longer promote abruptly to a particular broker, except you have got had been given a unique object that you desire to sell thru public sale.

Also, it's far a better know-how of buying the contemporary-day trouble of the Greysheet, the Coin Dealer Newsletter an excellent manner to, of course, provide you with a higher know-how of the overall marketplace.

Generally, your dealer will pay a bid or a small under bid for great coins that with out problem promote, and a lesser quantity for coins is taking extra time to sell due to the truth the lower-forestall coin collector. A terrific way of identifying the amount provider will pay for a coin you need to promote to see the web sites for some most vital shops, who at instances put up their searching for charges for objects they require.

Lastly, undergo in thoughts that many human beings do not understand that the coin marketplace is rotational and calls for time to make a earnings.

It is needed that one be affected man or woman, test the marketplace nicely, and remember that whilst you reason to maximise your go back, you will be required to hesitate for the marketplace so that your precise object can be superior.

Chapter 9: Detecting Counterfeited Coins

The dishonesty and artwork of counterfeit coins have been in life considering historical artisans first minted cash in 600BC. At first, people counterfeited cash due to the reality they favored to misinform citizens and consumers with the currently circulated fake cash. In state-of-the-art times, counterfeiters have created counterfeit coins to mislead creditors protecting favored cash no greater minted. However, a counterfeiter gets his cash with the useful

resource of taking fewer valuable materials and turning them into a few difficulty greater treasured.

Meaning of Counterfeit Coins?

Any coin created with the aid of any person without the approval and know-how of the issuing entity or u.S. Is called a counterfeited coin. In addition, normal cash might be transformed to be like a luxurious coins. In idea, no matter the fact that this isn't always counterfeiting, it is referred to as deceptive. Fraudulent human beings always boom new techniques to counterfeit cash. It is crook to create "replica" coins from a completely unique usa in China, and they continuously realise contemporary and stronger counterfeiting techniques.

A primary set of capabilities to choose out out counterfeited coins will likely save you some coins with the useful resource of evading the searching for of counterfeit cash. If you may spend some cheap quantity of forex on a coin, its higher you defend your self thru adhering to the following pointers:

•Only buy the cash that a 3rd-party grading facility has legal.

•Build a relationship with a well-knowledgeable coin provider and buy the coins from the provider.

•Do not buy any bargained cash furnished at flea markets and online systems.

•If you experience any coin is counterfeited, get recommendation from a next opinion earlier than looking for it.

Counterfeited Coins Types

Counterfeited coins might be classified into 3 components: Cast Counterfeits, altered cash, and struck counterfeits.

1. Cast Counterfeits

A an awful lot lots less-expensive manner of creating a counterfeit coin is to shape a mold of the real coin and use it to forged a counterfeit coin. To form the mildew is one manner or the opportunity honest. The host coin is used for example to create the solid. Counterfeiters select this technique due to the fact the manner does no longer damage the precept coin. The molten steel is poured into the mould when the molds are successfully available. Counterfeiters with greater revel in will use a centrifuge to make sure the molten metallic flows to the extreme breaks of the mold. Irrespective of the method of casting used, a low-rate counterfeit is constantly the very last results. Cast counterfeit cash are the most effects full-size counterfeit cash amongst all.

2. Altered and Doctored Coins

The fastest and much much much less-luxurious way of being profitable is even as you misinform a coin collector to take a regular coin and trade it to appear to be an uncommon and costly coin. For instance, a counterfeiter should buy a 1909 Lincoln cent with the designer's V.D.B. Initials on the decrease again for $20. A counterfeiter who is an professional can then include an S mint mark to the the the front and make the coin seem valued for over $1,000.

A one-of-a-type technique to modify the coin is to do away with a small detail to make it properly well worth appreciably sufficient cash. A dishonest person with little information can take a 1928-S peace dollar and take away the S mintmark. This can increase the coin's value thru tenfold.

A Split coin is a first rate kind of coin that has been truly altered. The counterfeit will take not unusual double coins, cut up them into halves, and solder or glue them collectively. This technique will result in a coin on the way to offer the affect of a greater luxurious and unusual coin. For example, a Buffalo nickel minted in 1926 at the Philadelphia mint may be offered for beneath $one hundred. A unique Buffalo nickel minted in 1929 on the San Francisco mint moreover may be offered for under $100. An skilled counterfeiter can divide the 2 cash into identical halves and use the the front of the 1926 nickel with the lower lower back of the 1929 nickel from San

Francisco and form a 1926-S Buffalo nickel in reality really worth like $10,000.

three. Struck Counterfeits

Counterfeiters create struck counterfeited coins in a comparable technique; a mint produces a actual coin via a planchet amongst coin dies in a coining press. The counterfeiter should make the coin dies thru inscribing them with the hands, with a one-to-one transmission inscribing lathe, the use of a plating method, spark erosion method or the effective method. Any of those strategies can bring about a totally deceptive counterfeit coin.

The counterfeiter now piles the coin dies proper into a coining press that uses super heaps of stress in putting the counterfeited cash. This production way is the maximum high-priced and most tough way to shape a counterfeit coin. Hence, the greater greater precious cash are counterfeited with the struck counterfeit method. More these days, counterfeited 1 pound cash from Great Britain were recognized.

How to Improve the Counterfeit Detection Skills

Various extraordinary counterfeit coins have even deceived professional numismatists. It is imperative to recognize the minting gadget for the outstanding coins you look at. For instance, the primary cash fashioned on the U.S Mint had been constructed from coin dies that have been one after the other hand-engraved with the resource of using a sketcher. When the die broke or wore out, the artist makes a few different one. Though cash may be of a similar denomination and date, cash crafted from each special hand-crafted coin dies may have dissimilarities.

The U.S Mint presented its first decreasing lathe in 1833. The lathe have become the primary diploma to automate the manufacturing of coin dies to make certain there are layout stabilities for the complete production 12 months. A coin made because of the truth the three hundred and sixty five days starts offevolved with one coin die might likely almost differentiate from a coin produced at the stop of the 12 months the use of some exceptional die set. Nevertheless, a few discrepancies despite the fact that occurred with this manual technique.

The present day minting technique now uses hydraulic presses, computerized techniques, and computer systems to make sure that each coin is almost tremendous from the following ones. These advances have made cutting-edge cash extra hard to counterfeit.

Chapter 10: What Is Numismatics?

Numismatics is the look at of coins, medals, and tokens.

According to the most notably normal definition, it's far the systematic series and have a look at of cash. It is characterized as coin collecting in a completely slim experience.

Numismatics usually consists of the check of any steel that has been used by the people of a specific technology or time in records.

Numismatists are coin creditors who have a look at the sector of numismatics. People interested in Ancient Greek or Roman coins, medieval or hammered cash, and modern-day-day struck cash are normal of this organization.

It gives the opportunity of analyzing the records and the way of life of numerous 0.33 worldwide worldwide places. For instance, to test the historic cash found in Anatolia, you have to visit Turkey. To check

American coins, you will should excursion to the united statesA.

You can also get specific offers on your buddies as it's now not very expensive. The monetary, social, political, cultural, and aesthetic dispositions of the on the spot are contemplated in numismatics. If there's a excessive name for for them, their intrinsic numismatic fee also can rise above their present day rate.

Numismatics permits you to shop for cash reasonably-priced and promote high priced. If you buy an historic coin properly really worth 10 $, and its fee rises, you can sell it off in income. But if you located that money within the economic institution, you may never be capable of make a income like this.

It's additionally a manner of making an investment because it gives remarkable returns compared to a few distinct investment subject.

While numismatic substances which includes the Ancient Greek or Roman cash, medieval or hammered coins, and modern struck cash are normally valued for monetary and business organisation price, in addition they have got huge historical and progressive price.

Coins also are crucial and valued in archeology due to the fact they mirror the those who minted them or the time they have been coined.

Numismatics is also developing very speedy as a hobby inside the beyond few years because of the Internet, social networks, and the Internet in extensive.

Brief History of Coins and Coin Collection

Coins were round considering that historical instances, in which they had been manufactured from treasured metals. Today, some coins are though made from treasured metal, however current coins are made regularly of aluminum, copper, or nickel. During historical instances, they have been used because the jail technique of fee.

The term, Numismatics; coin accumulating as we apprehend it, is derived from the Greek word "nomisma," which means "criminal cash or coin." While we now use checks, paper payments, and, an increasing number of, credit score playing playing cards for our every day charges, ancient societies tailored coins as their fee tool.

Lydia in Asia Minor, that's now part of Turkey however grow to be beneath Greek affect at the time, created the earliest cash recognized to had been minted. They have a 2,600year-vintage records. They used Gold and silver alloy to make the number one cash.

The Lydians have been corporation-minded human beings on the time. They may additionally moreover need to create a rich civilization that advanced trade, economic tool, and trade. This era's cash show how coin format has advanced through the years.

Gold and silver ingots have been the maximum famous sorts of charge in the path of the length. Because there had been no requirements and plenty of dishonest merchants, each transaction regarding gold and silver charge necessitated an correct weighing of the medium.

Around 650 B.C., cash had been invented, and that they've been struck with standardized gold and silver weights. The authorities branded it with a charge assure. The development of coinage as a number one medium of alternate befell inside the subsequent century.

Numismatics or Coin collection is considered to have commenced with the first coin. Because there had been no banks on the time, accumulating them seemed like an brilliant way to hold them strong. They had been being stockpiled for his or her inherent fee as well as their rarity. These cash had been passed down through the generations as a family heirloom.

According to three researchers, actual coin collecting originated within the overdue Middle Ages, even as severa European kings searched and acquired specific cash used as coins thru historical societies. They observed that no cash had been similar due to the numerous procedures used to strike the cash. Coins had been struck with the aid of hand then, and it wasn't till the 1500s that device-minted cash have turn out to be famous. This interest is commonly called the "Hobby of Royalty" because it began out out with European kings gathering cash.

During the Renaissance, coin collecting have grow to be popular, and masses of formidable people began to make a plethora of remarkable counterfeit. Because in their outstanding, antiquity, and historic importance, even those forgeries were given a excessive-price these days.

1st Copper Coins

The first copper coins have been minted in the United States in 1793 as part of the Coinage Act, and they had been made on the Philadelphia Mint. At the time, production have grow to be finished with the useful resource of hand, and every coin changed into struck one after the opposite. On March three, 1835, the authorities devised a mint marking device to differentiate cash synthetic in every branch.

Rules dominated the identification of cash stamped at every unit. They were speculated to make certain that each one coinage changed into underneath their supervision and that coinage output became uniform across the board.

Countries which incorporates Italy, France, Rome, China, Japan, and Austria all minted cash into movement all through the ones ancient instances.

Modern Numismatics

The have a have a observe of coins from the mid-seventeenth to the twenty-first century is cutting-edge numismatics. Machines first minted cash during this era. Modern numismatics caters to creditors and amateur enthusiasts; although, historical cash attracted the eye of professional researchers, historians, and archeologists due to their historical and archeological rate.

Modern Numismatics is worried with identifying the relative rarity based on its production and use. Coin versions, mint-made mistakes, the effect of present day die put on, mint markings, and figures are some of the other subjects of hobby in current-day numismatics.

The American Numismatic Society (A.N.S.), an international non-profits commercial enterprise employer dedicated to maintaining and analyzing coins and other numismatic artifacts together with medals and paper cash, changed into primarily based in 1858 by using a collection of creditors.

Coins with historical significance, mint errors, confined versions, and commemorative coins are the numerous maximum sought through contemporary coin creditors. In this regard, mastering a way to grade coins effectively is one of the most valuable abilties a coin collector can have.

How Coins Are Made- The Minting Process

Coins are genuinely quite clean — they have simply stamped metal discs. Yet their simplicity belies a quite complicated and well-organized manner that takes years and hundreds of human beings to execute.

If you're new to coin accumulating, getting to know how coins are artificial will assist you draw near the diverse types of coins to be had. It will supply an purpose of why a few cash are uncirculated at the identical time as others are called resistant cash.

Ancient Coins:

Artisans have been manufacturing everything from domestic items to agricultural device in ancient instances. Making cash modified into taken into consideration certainly one of their obligations. They employed minimal gadgets, and the final consequences changed into often relying on their capabilities. The terrific of the struck cash varies, from Palestine's "widow's mite" to Greek Sicily's awesome silver portions.

An oven for heating blanks or "flans," tongs, an anvil located on a desk or bench, and 2 dies for impressing the layout into the flan were the primary gadgets used by the artisans. Dies were crafted from tough bronze or iron. Bronze corroded extra speedy than silver, even though it become less complicated to engrave and no longer tarnish.

Chapter 11: Modern United States Coins

In the US, current-day-technology cash started out inside the non-public region. Some coinage blanks, planchets, and particular materials offered with the resource of manner of the U.S. Mint were made through non-public businesses. In 1792, the U.S. Congress passed the Coinage Act, which set up the united states Mint as a part of the U.S. Treasury Department. Many distant places and colonial currencies were used before it.

The new law mandated the hooked up order of a country extensive mint in Philadelphia, the united states's capital at the time. The United States Mint is in rate of producing, promoting, and safeguarding the u . S . A .'s foreign cash and belongings. Between 14 and 28 billion bypass cash are produced every year, and sixty five to eighty million cash are minted each day as of 2004. Only coins produced via the us Mint are time-venerated as jail coins within the United States.

All materials had to make U.S. Cash are supplied from business companies. The U.S. Mint receives pre-made one-cent coin blanks however creates five-cent coin blanks and cupronickel clad coins from the strip.

The manufacturing technique is largely the equal for all denominations. Dimes, quarters, half of of dollars, and dollars, however, go through a technique called "reeding," which leaves microscopic ridges on the coins. These ridges save you the precious metal in gold and silver coins from being illegally shaved or clipped. It may additionally moreover furthermore not be crucial, but it is being finished to honor an prolonged-standing technique extending over again to colonial instances. It's moreover to useful resource visually impaired humans in spotting the cash.

All circulating coins need to go through the inscriptions "Liberty," "In God We Trust," "The United States of America," and "E Pluribus Unum," further to the denomination and 12 months of issuance, as required by regulation. Since 1909, the slogan "In God We Trust" has been on the best-cent overseas cash, and because of the fact that 1916, on the 10-cent denomination. All gold and silver dollar cash, 1/2 of-dollar cash, and area coins started out to function this inscription on July 1, 1908.

Minting Process

Minting is the technique deemed as adding a ultra-cutting-edge coin to go together with the float or converting the feature of an current coin. Minting cash follows a sensitive gadget it is:

Blanking:

To make the nickel, dime, area, half of of of-dollar, and the dollar, the U.S. Mint purchases strips of metal which may be 13 inches massive and 1,500 ft lengthy. The strips are available in a coil shape. Each coil is handed right right into a blanking press, which punches out blanks, which may be round discs. Webbing, the leftover strip, is sliced and recycled. (After offering fabricators with copper and zinc, the Mint purchases organized-to-stamp blanks for the cent.)

Blanks are planchets that have now not surpassed through the popular processing strategies earlier than being struck into coins. A planchet is a clean that has completed all the important strategies and is ready to be pounded. These blanks are frequently large than finished cash. They characteristic burrs on the edges, which might be eliminated at a few diploma in the subsequent operations.

Annealing, washing, and drying:

To soften the blanks, they're heated in an annealing furnace. After that, they'll be placed thru a showering device and dryer.

The blanks harden due to the end rolling and blanking sports activities. They're cooked to round 1400 tiers Fahrenheit in a controlled environment. The annealing approach relaxes the crystal structure of the substances, making them less tough to art work on. The existence of the coining dies prolonged because of the decrease setting pressure.

On the blanks, the annealing system generates minor discoloration. The blanks are thrown toward one more and sent through a chemical bath to eliminate them. The blanks are then dried with pressurized warm air, and if essential, components of them are transferred to the scary mill.

Ridding:

Ridding is the 1/3 step. The blanks are screened on "riddles" in advance than being dissatisfied to eliminate the incorrect length or form.

Upsetting:

The appropriate blanks are then run thru an frightening mill. A rim workplace work spherical their edges because of this.

The provoking mill includes a revolving wheel with a groove on one aspect that suits proper into a curving section with its very private track. The raised rim created at some degree within the technique sizes and office work the easy, permitting it to feed extra with out troubles through the clicking and hardening the brink, preventing metal from escaping the various obverse die and the collar.

Striking:

The blanks are then sent to the coining press. They are then stamped with the designs and inscriptions that understand them as actual U.S. Cash.

Inspecting:

Each batch of newly struck cash is spot-checked thru press operators using magnifying lenses.

Bagging and Counting:

Finally, the cash are counted and deposited into massive bags using an automated counting tool. The bags are sealed, positioned onto pallets, and transported to the vaults for garage. Trucks supply new coinage to Federal Reserve Banks. The cash are then introduced for your close by economic group!

Coin Distribution

The United States Mint is constantly enhancing its techniques for estimating coinage call for. This is to ensure that the movement of U.S. Coinage is green and consistent. The U.S. Mint plans production and coin distribution schedules the usage of economic factors and ancient seasonal tendencies. It's drastically implemented to calculate information related to coin manufacturing and distribution.

Because forecasting isn't correct, manufacturing want to account for potential deviations. The cash are commonly transported in armored tractor-trailer vehicles.

How are the cash allotted?

The distribution of coins within the U.S. Is completed through the Bureau of Engraving and Printing. They artwork with a agenda to offer cash at the identical time as they're wanted. The plan is primarily based at the call for for coins thru the overall public and organizations.

The Basics of Coin Collecting

Coin gathering is an amusing interest with a thriving network of lenders global. Coins are available in all patterns and sizes, with massive-ranging pursuits from precise Collectors.

Coin amassing can be a a laugh and worthwhile interest. There's a few problem continuously stunning about a piece of coins this is assessed at (regularly substantially) extra than its unique cost and moreover bears the information of its time.

Coins regularly depict royalty, terrific leaders, statistics, electricity, and patriotism. For example, historic coins depicted Julius Caesar and Alexander the Great; modern-day cash depict Henry VIII, Napoleon, George Washington, and Abraham Lincoln.

Chapter 12: How Do You Get Started, And In Which Do You Skip From There?

In this financial disaster, I've accumulated a number of the most important factors of coin amassing: the have to-haves to start with, further to the foundation guidelines upon that you need to broaden your collection. We'll cover some essential mind, like what coins are and the manner they're made.

I may also speak wherein to find out terrific forms of cash and a few functionality pitfalls if making a decision to start accumulating. It's time in your million-greenback concept!

Coin Collection: The Art, the Business and the Science

The pride and praise of coin collecting are extremely good from particular hobbies which include stamping or paper cash. Coin accumulating has a wealthy records and can be treasured to the extreme collector.

The interest or industrial organization of Coin Collecting calls for staying energy, know-how, and a deep know-how of the cash you accumulate. Most coin collectors are passionate about the statistics, rarity, and form of coins they collect.

For example, the primary Flowing Hair Silver Dollar emerge as minted in 1794 and is currently valued at $10 million. And this is not an remoted incident. People have made fortunes off of pennies through the years. As a quit quit end result, it is smooth to appearance why such masses of human beings are inquisitive about coin gathering and what it includes.

However, coin amassing is plenty more than that. It is an artwork—absolutely as collecting artwork is an act of creativity in and of itself (if that makes any enjoy).

Coin collecting is also fascinating from a systematic and ancient perspective. Everyone should be aware of specific "technicalities" before beginning to accumulate cash, as you'll see sooner or later of this ebook. But do not worry; the ones technicalities may be interesting, I promise.

Coin collecting began out as a seemingly natural and affordable conduct: people stored their excessive-charge cash (along side those crafted from silver or gold) and spent their lower-value ones. People started to accumulate coins for their aesthetic attraction as nicely over the years. For example, many humans have end up inquisitive about vintage Roman cash at some level in the Renaissance (which moreover attracted some of forgeries into the "enterprise").

The 1893 World Columbian Exposition, which additionally featured a commemorative U.S. Dollar coin, heralded the begin of contemporary-day coin amassing. Coin accumulating has risen in reputation in the course of the twentieth century, with a pointy surge in interest inside the remaining three a long term.

Refined gentlemen in Victorian times took pride in collecting as a minimum a small series of antiques (which often blanketed coins as nicely). The interest become already famous and famous, so it was first-class a be counted of time in advance than it attracted more devotees.

The variety of coin creditors inside the United States is unknown (or the place, in truth). However, a few estimates recommend that as many as ten million people are engaged in coin amassing (pleasant inside the U.S.).

On the opportunity hand, Coin amassing need to no longer be taken into consideration a get-wealthy-quick scam in any manner. Yes, coin collections can make you hundreds of coins, but the reality is that the ones uncommon reveals need big investment and hundreds of labor.

Before you even start reading approximately the subtleties of coin amassing, make sure you are familiar with the two primary sorts of people who are interested by it.

All Coin lenders fall under the primary type. These acquire numerous coins and sort them into classes primarily based absolutely totally on their alternatives. For instance: era, presidents, united states of america, and plenty of others.

Numismatic specialists fall into the second one kind. The maximum first rate distinction amongst them and the previous business enterprise, Coin Collectors, is that they technique coin gathering greater methodically. They could have a observe a coin, confirm its validity, and trace its statistics, production, and substances once more to its very origins.

In addition, numismatics is a subject that encompasses coin technological information and studies and the have a look at of the whole lot that can be used as a form of overseas cash, which consist of token payments, medals, and tokens.

Although all numismatists are coin creditors in some techniques, not all coin lenders are numismatists.

Furthermore, at the same time as coin creditors form clubs, numismatists are more likely to be related with authentic establishments that target their place of observe.

Here are the numerous maximum well-known numismatists' agencies from subsequently of the region:

•The Czech Numismatic Society, a non-profits business business enterprise organization committed to studying cash.

•The Guild of Ancient Coin Collectors

•The Royal Numismatic Society, a numismatic society primarily based absolutely genuinely inside the United Kingdom.

•America's Archeological Institute

Also, as you could expect, numerous of these companies location a pinnacle magnificence on the vicinity of their individuals or headquarters. On the alternative hand, others are laser-targeted on a specific location of hobby.

Who Collects Coins?

What can be a honest extra important fallacy to debunk is the definition of a coin collector? Coin amassing is regularly related with the rich, perhaps because of the picture of Victorian gents interested in antiques.

That isn't always the case, despite the fact that.

Coin collecting is now a interest that appeals to severa socioeconomic instructions, a long time, and cutting-edge pursuits. Everyone in recent times may be a coin collector, from children to grandparents, engineers to artists, and guys to girls.

Who is it that gathers coins in recent times?

Any of the following education can be the case:

A conventional hunter will normally exit searching with a listing and make sure he sticks to it. The collector is well-prepared and ordinary, and they'll regularly now not stop till they have got checked off all of the items or cash on their to-do listing.

The aesthetic collector is in elegant interested in coins which have a pleasant appearance. The appearance of these cash is sometimes more giant to this form of collector than their evaluated price.

A speculator will best accumulate to growth the price of his funding. As a famous rule, I ought to not suggest you to try this, especially as a novice. Coin amassing can be about a excellent deal more than in truth income.

The perfectionist will in no manner prevent looking for best cash in each manner. They want the coin to appear ideal, to be treasured, and to be in wonderful shape.

The good deal or cheap collector will need to accumulate as hundreds as feasible and continuously look for a bargain. His primary interest is affordability, and he's going to hoard coins without a doubt because of the reality they may be very cheaper.

The presenter is the form of collector that does such things as this to brag about his series. In his home, he's going to create a entire altar for his cash, and he's going to not leave out an event to expose them off to every person he brings over.

Sometimes, the academic collector is likewise a numismatist (as a minimum at the amateur degree). He'll amass now not first-class cash however moreover a wealth of information approximately them, to the point that he may be able to create a ebook at the priority.

Historian creditors will accumulate coins on the grounds that they will be historical artifacts. Coins are dwelling testaments to a bygone era. This type of collector may also have an nearly emotional bond collectively along with his cash.

The patriot will mainly accumulate cash related to his usa of the us's beyond. Most of the time, the same character might moreover collect different artifacts regarding his area of start.

Of route, you could become a collector who does not suit nicely into any of the companies referred to above. The thing of discussing them end up now not that will help you "pick out out" a typology but to show you that there are various precise styles of coin creditors. This is a hobby that nearly anyone can experience.

Chapter 13: Kind Of Coins

There are a few matters to maintain in thoughts at the equal time as starting a coin collection. Of route, you're unfastened to preserve in any way you notice healthy. Finally, coin collecting want to be a hobby—however, as every body understand, interests aren't usually nicely prepared and categorised.

Suppose you want to get out on the proper foot and make gathering treasured cash in severa verticals a whole lot less tough in the destiny. In that case, you want to conform with the hints in this bankruptcy. Hopefully, on the give up of it, you can have determined out the whole thing there may be to recognise about prepping for your foray into the precious international of coin collecting.

Different Kinds of Coins

Coins are to be had in lots of specific styles and sizes, which include round and rectangular. They moreover function certainly one of a kind colours on their surfaces, which includes gold and silver.

Different standards can be used to classify cash (which includes the material used for making them, as an example, or the occasion on which they have been created). To make subjects less complex for you, we won't cross into too much element about the proper instructions. Instead, we are capable of gift you with the most commonplace coin types and terms in sizable.

Gold and Silver Coin:

Since historical instances, maximum worldwide places have used gold and silver coins. These international places encompass Ancient Rome, Ancient Greece, Egypt, England, and america.

Gold Coins:

Gold Coins are quite terrific. They're well really worth extra than every one of a kind steel, they will be used to maintain wealth, and they will be in reality cool searching.

Gold does not exist in its natural shape. With normal mining strategies, it's miles not feasible to discover sufficient for what might be taken into consideration a big amount of gold due to the fact it is so unusual. That's why most gold is placed within the ground in the veins of numerous minerals.

These veins are deep inside the Earth, lots of feet down. The rock from which the ones tiny veins are fashioned is referred to as quartz, and it is loaded with gold. The gold itself is mixed with particular metals and minerals surrounding it. These greater minerals embody iron, copper, silver, and positive kinds of treasured stones like diamonds (regardless of the truth that diamonds and quartz have a propensity to stick together as they're near loved ones).

Gold has constantly been a perfect funding, and now that the fee of gold is the least bit-time highs, it's far lots more so. When human beings consider gold, they normally consider bars. Still, gold coins have other benefits, which encompass monetary viability and modest denominations.

Silver Coin:

Silver cash may be used as a medium of exchange. Still, they're greater regularly used as a shop of fee due to their inherent rarity relative to paper coins or distinct metals which include gold.

Silver coins are extra ordinary in international locations wherein their float is prison. They are notably taken into consideration to show off better value than extraordinary coins with similar or lesser usage. They additionally have an vital position in exchange and a minor form of physical remote places cash. In some times, silver is minted for coinage.

Coins generally produced for that reason are 90% natural ("bullion") silver or ninety% base material with out a various factors (which include copper) protected improving the appearance of the coin. However, there are a few times wherein silver coins have been struck to better purity requirements.

Gold and silver coins aren't applied in normal transactions, however lenders pretty are trying to find them. Depending on what form of gold or silver coin you are looking for, the price of such a piece may be incredibly immoderate.

Commemorative Coins

Commemorative cash feature a design on one trouble to commemorate a person, occasion, or motive that is huge to a selected america or region. They function a souvenir and tangible reminder of the significance of the occasion being celebrated.

The use of commemorative coins dates another time to historic times. The historic Greeks and Romans used cash with pix of the emperors and critical historic sports activities, including battles and gladiators' battles. Today, commemorative cash are restrained to best the Greeks and Romans. Still, maximum cultures spherical the region have particular designs.

The first wave of commemorative coins drew many people into coin accumulating, and that they hold to carry out that these days. Commemorative coins are appealing and elegant to coin creditors and those who are not interested in coin gathering in large.

Revolutionary Coins:

Revolutionary coins, in a nutshell, are coins that circulated at some point of instances of revolution (at the side of the American Revolution of 1776, for example). These cash may be precious because of their historical importance (but this depends on various factors).

Ancient Coins:

In the current, cash are a common remote places cash used by many nations global. But at the same time as they will now not be ancient in shape, they have got an exciting data that dates lower decrease returned to a number of the earliest civilizations in lifestyles, like the ones decided in historical Mesopotamia or Egypt.

Ancient coins are often stressed with gold and silver coinage. However, this isn't always the case, as miners applied first-rate substances to make coins in the beyond (which embody glass, ivory, or porcelain, for example).

Another common misconception concerning historical coins is that they may be prohibitively high priced. While this will be right in some cases, you could nonetheless non-public one (or extra) with out breaking the bank because of the reality a coin's marketplace cost is not quality advocated by using using its age.

Another not unusual false impression regarding historical coins is that they may be prohibitively steeply-priced. However, on the same time as this may be actual in some instances, you could although non-public one (or more) without breaking the financial institution due to the reality a coin's market charge isn't always only caused with the aid of way of its age.

Souvenir Pennies:

These cash have pretty a few potentials. They're regular cash which have been pressed, stretched, and changed somehow. The most interesting element about them is that mutilating cash to position them again into movement is banned except for those memento pennies. Souvenir Pennies make a fun addition to any collector's series!

Medallions:

The time period "medallion" is frequently used to signify a full-size sort of cash (which incorporates commemorative coins). In preferred, "medallions" speak over with any spherical, ornamented piece of metallic with a few importance related to it (inclusive of financial rate, as an example). On the opportunity hand, actual medallions are not often determined via felony clean.

Coin medallions are well-known amongst creditors, jewelers, and those interested in numismatics because of the fact they will be valuable. However, it might assist in case you seemed past the charge of a coin medallion. Overall awesome want to be your primary attention whilst buying this sort of coins.

Tokens

Trade tokens are scarce and precious collectibles. They can be well definitely well worth severa loads of bucks in some cases (e.G., Civil War tokens, for example).

Typically, those tokens had been made in some unspecified time in the destiny of financial trouble even as silver and gold have been uncommon. However, People despite the fact that required a form of price.

Tokens were frequently for $1 or less at face charge, however the truth that a few tokens can be honestly really worth as masses as $5. They were utilized in everyday transactions much like "notable" bypass coins.

The location of knowledge of coin tokens is that they need now not be redeemed right now or inner any unique duration. Coin tokens may be traded simplest with different buyers who hold them as non-redeemable stock or cash. This way that they will be separated from every considered one of a type.

Error Coins:

They occur on the equal time as there can be an mistakes in producing those cash (including a double denomination, over the date, or brokerage). They came out of the mint in this condition, and a few can be persuaded to bear in mind they may be nugatory. On the alternative hand, blunders coins may be pretty high-priced relying on the flaw and their era.

Error cash, in great, may be described as a coin this is in a few manner defective. Whether the error inside the coin is because of damage or tooling, or layout faults, it's going to have an impact on its fee.

Types of Errors in cash embody:

•Dies - cash struck on the wrong planchet or planchets that do not in shape dies.

•Hammering - wherein a coin's die is broken each via the use of tooling or at a few stage in the coin's production.

•Striking - in which there are troubles with a coin's striking.

•Clashing - in which there was an problem with how dies were used collectively to make a milled coin.

B.U. Rolls:

B.U. Rolls are emblematic of the new era of coin lenders that emerged on the quit of the Nineteen Fifties and Nineteen Sixties. These "rolls" had been economic institution-wrapped Brilliant Uncirculated little stashes of coins that drove lenders insane at some stage within the duration. Collectors located out that, despite the fact that some of those B.U.Rolls have been represented as uncommon, they were quite common, and their 15-minute glory started out to wane (because of the reality the tens of tens of tens of millions had synthetic them). As a give up end result, B.U. Rolls are frequently startlingly low in rate in recent times, so that you may additionally need to keep away from falling proper right into a trap with them.

Silver Certificates:

Silver certificates are a type of obligation subsidized via using the united states government. People achieved antique Silver Certificates to exchange one silver greenback. These certificate, but, were great legitimate until 1964, at the same time as the government stopped producing them. For a time, despite the fact that, customers must alternate their silver certificate for a sure quantity of silver, which spawned an entire new coin gathering mania.

Because mintages have been initially limited, art bars were as an alternative excellent. However, the marketplace have become saturated with those art work bars, and customers in the end have grow to be tired of them.

Chapter 14: What Makes Coins Valuable?

Coins had been making their manner spherical civilization for masses of years now, and the idea of cash has changed greater than as soon as in that point. However, irrespective of how an entire lot the fee of cash changes and how often they go through or provide you with a trendy concept of coins, they remain the most valuable factor humans can use in change for gadgets and services.

However, to apprehend why the ones cash are properly really worth masses, you need to first take a look at out the traits which cause them to precious.

Characteristics of Coins to Consider

Name of the denomination: Different denominations are issued through each foreign cash (which includes the penny, the nickel, the dime, and the place, for instance).

Type: This does no longer continuously exercise to the coin sorts top notch inside the preceding phase of our e book however rather to the designs to be had for each denomination. Coins should be recognized thru their layout and not with out trouble incorrect for each other coin kind.

Issue date: Some humans favor to accumulate coins based totally on the date they were released, this is completely OK. For example, you would probable choice to collect all kinds of nickels minted among 1900 to the triumphing.

Year: This collection shape includes all cash released throughout your starting yr.

Coins with the identical date and mintmark: You can also need to accumulate cash with the same date and mintmark. Keep in mind that this can be more high-priced than in truth ordering them in keeping with their technology, as most coin series feature a completely precious mintmark.

Based on the ones features, what makes these coins as valuable are:

•The weight modern-day for the whole coin denomination.

•The content fabric cloth and charge of the steel used on the coin.

•How regularly have been the coins minted, and what number of pieces were stamped that three hundred and sixty 5 days.

A coin's criminal mild recognition.

All of those may additionally moreover seem difficult in case you are certainly getting started together along side your coin gathering. But do not worry; if you are curious and take a look at as hundreds as you can on the hassle, you may examine the whole lot there is to recognize approximately this beneficial hobby in this ebook.

The Vocabulary of Coin Collecting

The coin collection has its lingo. While this is not a complete list of each coin amassing time period you can encounter, it does consist of meanings for the maximum extensively used terms.

Alloy

Cupro-nickel or cupro-zinc coins have a mixture of or more metals.

Ancient

Any coin struck earlier than 500 A.D. Is referred to as a "pre-500" coin.

Bag Marks

Nicks, scuffs, and scratches because of coins colliding in a mint bag.

Bi-Metallic Coin

A coin with a unmarried steel within the middle and a incredible metal within the outer half.

Blank

A piece of round steel intended to be minted into overseas cash later.

Bullion

Bullion is gold or certainly one of a type treasured metallic cash with little numismatic nicely properly well worth other than the current price of the metallic it's miles made from.

Cameo

A coin that has a frosty look.

Circulated Coin

A coin that has been used as remote places cash and has some placed on.

Commemorative Coin

A coin providing a format commemorating a historical or gift occasion, a famous parent, or a notable anniversary.

Error Coin

A coin that has been produced mistakenly or with a unique design than intended.

Grade

A prescribed approach determines a coin's scenario.

High Points

the fine element of a coin's layout, wherein the number one traces of wear and tear and tear are generally seen.

Legend

The phrases are engraved all through the outside vicinity; the legend inscription on U.S. Cash is E Pluribus Unum.

Mintage

The widespread fashion of coins produced thru a mint in a given denomination, date, and/or type.

Mint Mark

A sign that identifies the mint that created the coin.

Mint State

An uncirculated coin in fine circumstance, without a traces of damage as whilst it come to be produced.

Numismatics

The take a look at of cash, paper cash, tokens, medals, and distinctive gadgets of a similar nature.

Obverse

A portrait of a president, king, queen, or different country wide chief seems on the "heads" thing of the coin.

Proof Coins

Coins struck with greater strain than ordinary the use of in particular polished dies to provide a more pretty polished or reflect-like format

Reverse

The all over again or "tails" issue of a coin, the alternative issue of the obverse facet of a coin.

Rim

The rim of a coin.

Un-circulated coin

A coin that has in no manner been used as cash and has no apparent signs and symptoms of harm.

Variety

Any trade within the layout of a coin results within the advent of a modern day coin kind.

We will attempt to define extra terminologies as they seem on this e-book, but that could be a decent vicinity to start for the beginner collector.

Handling and Cleaning Your Coins

Handling

In preferred, collector cash should be treated with care to avoid placed on or the introduction of materials that could motive spots or color modifications. Many holders will supply sufficient protection for normal coping with but count on two times in advance than casting off a coin from its holder.

Only the threshold of an uncirculated or evidence coin need to be touched. Fingerprints on my own have the capacity to decrease the coin's grade and, as a end result, its charge. When reading another individual's coins, you need to continually address them on aspect regardless of grade. If you get into the exercising of choosing up collectible cash through their edges, it turns into second nature.

Holding numismatic gadgets in the front of your mouth isn't a extraordinary idea. Little particles of moisture can motive spots.

Place a coin on a clean, clean floor even as setting it down outdoor a holder. A velvet pad is an wonderful floor for dealing with valuable substances regularly. A easy, soft cloth or blank piece of paper may additionally moreover suffice for a good deal less valued subjects. No coins should be dragged for the duration of any surfaces.

Wearing a smooth white fabric or surgical gloves and a masks may be important if you are coping with specially costly coins or many uncirculated or higher grade circulated cash.

Cleaning Coins

In most occasions, it isn't always essential to smooth coins. While you may count on that colourful cash seem higher, creditors decide on coins with their specific appearance. Cleaning a coin can halve or in all likelihood greater than halve its collector charge.

Like overhauling works of artwork, cleaning coins is satisfactory left to specialists who've the understanding and experience to determine at the same time as it's far suitable, which strategies will art work quality, and the manner to rent them efficiently.

Suppose making a decision to visit the hassle, never clean cash with abrasive cleaners. Even scrubbing the coin with a sensitive fabric can leave little however large scratches, decreasing the coin's rate.

It is better to go away a coin by myself if the surface seems to be tarnished. A natural system stated to creditors as firming is chargeable for the coloration shift. Chemical reactions have happened on the coin's floor, maximum commonly with sulfur compounds. It isn't always possible to opposite the reaction.

There are "dips" available, which dispose of molecules off the floor. Dipping is the right instance of a way that, if achieved the least bit, need to only be finished via experts.

Natural firming also can improve a coin's properly well worth.

Dirt and other overseas materials caught to a coin can be eliminated in some times. You can soak the coin in olive oil or soapy water for some days, then rinse it thoroughly with tap water. Allow the coin to air dry or use compressed air to dry it. The coin need to no longer be rubbed. Commercial coin cleaners can also be used to launch remote places materials extra rapid.

Hairlines will seem on a coin that has been wiped clean using an abrasive. Abrasive cleansing can also leave a few debris in the coin's crevices.

It may additionally moreover moreover or may not be detectable if the coin has been dipped. It's viable that an actual coin exists, although it's great. Dipping also can get rid of the shine from the coin.

A herbal coin has a outstanding look that presentations its storage records. The toning of haphazardly stored coins has a "dirty" appearance. Coins which have been in a coin cabinet for a long time normally display off adorable coloured firming.

Coins stored in a easy metallic vault (which includes an vintage-fashion "piggy" bank) can ultimate a long time and continue to be white (or pink). Coins in albums each increase "ring toning" or "one-sided toning," it actually is a ways much less appealing. Coins stored in mint bags regularly show off excellent rainbow firming, similar to that discovered in coin shelves.

Coins made from copper, bronze, or brass which have been wiped clean have an synthetic tint, comparable to a toned gold coin. Even once they've been re-toned, they're but uneven and feature an uncommon shade. The presence of pink in the recesses of that V.F. Copper coin isn't a brilliant indicator. The copper that has been honestly toned and *circulated* has a quite uniform color. However, it may be darkish and dusty in the course of the lettering and other covered locations. Uncirculated copper (especially proofs) can also have an uneven tone, so do not dismiss this form of coin robotically.

Silver coins that have been wiped clean and re-toned, alternatively, have a tendency to be tremendously constant in coloration, together with the tops of the inscriptions and protected areas. Silver coins with herbal firming will usually show a few shade variant at those places. Be conscious that a uniform slate grey hue can be without problem completed on silver using plenty of chemical materials. Finally, a heavily toned after which dipped silver coin could have a gray look delivered approximately via surface roughness in preference to tarnish. A close examination with a amazing magnifier can display this.

Chapter 15: How To Handle Coins

A cardinal rule for all coin creditors is to avoid causing placed on or introducing any materials which can cause spots or shade adjustments. Try to avoid any direct manual contact collectively together with your cash. This way no longer the usage of your bare fingers to deal with the coins. Fingerprints are collectible coin's sworn enemies. It is likewise crucial to make certain which you do not permit one coin contact some other coin due to the truth it is able to bring about nicks and scratches. To avoid ruining them, take away coins from their garage boxes best while definitely desired and vital.

Uncirculated or Proof cash ought to no longer be treated anywhere but the issue, as even a moderate fingerprint may additionally lessen its grade and, eventually, its rate. Proof cash are struck or greater times with polished dyes on an further polished planchet; they will be jail mild like normal cash.

Uncirculated mint gadgets are cash packaged by manner of manner of the U.S. Authorities in the marketplace to coin creditors. It is great if you make it a dependancy to pick up collectible coins via their edges even as carrying smooth white cotton or surgical gloves. A face mask is likewise pinnacle-rated to prevent small particles of moisture which can purpose undesirable spots. Never sneeze or cough close to cash due to the fact this can without a doubt go away marks and wreck the coin.

Mint Coins

Coin holders provide enough protection for ordinary managing. If you want to take the coin out and want to area it down outside the holder, make sure you location it on a smooth and soft floor, preferably a velvet pad. It is a splendid surface and a must-have for dealing with treasured numismatic materials. For cash with lesser fee, a smooth, gentle fabric can be used. Avoid dragging cash on any floor to avoid scratches. Take be aware that even wiping with a easy cloth can motive scratches that reduce its price.

You want to examine severa guidelines at the same time as considering cleansing the coins you've got truely obtained, placed, sold or inherited.

1.Never smooth a coin that you do not understand the numismatic charge

of. If you doubt if it's far precious or now not, then do no longer clean it every. It is amazing to go away coins the way you determined them, untouched. Erring at the conservative aspect is maximum popular to ruining the coin for no longer whatever. Store them in holders made for the purpose. Coin lenders and sellers opt for coins in their real situation to not modify their country. Cleaning will likely do more damage than appropriate.

2.Because you aren't presupposed to smooth the coins your self, then you actually want to take the cash to a expert coin cleaning service. They use a manner known as

"dipping" with a purpose to properly smooth the cash with out decreasing their fee. This is critical specially if the coin's date and statistics can't be determined due to corrosion. A expert will recognize a way to avoid or lessen in addition damage to the coin.

3. In the situation that you need to easy the coin you have got located, then do it with the least dangerous approach. Do now not use harsh chemical materials, sulfuric acid, sharpening material,

vinegar, abrasive pastes, or gadgets that provide the coin a smooth and colourful end result. Experiment first with lesser cost coins earlier than coins with immoderate fee.

Cleaning is a big trouble in coin amassing, so that you have to disclose this reality to a client if you are promoting a coin that you understand has been wiped easy.

Soaking coin

Cleaning Different Types of Coins

Uncirculated coins – have to never be cleaned in any respect due to the fact cleansing will wreck any mint luster.

Gold Coins – ought to be washed cautiously in easy, warmth soapy distilled water using a fluffy cotton washcloth or a very smooth toothbrush. Gold is a mild metal, so that you need to take more care to keep away from disfiguring or scratching.

Martha Washington Gold Coin

Silver Coins – precious silver cash want to not be wiped easy in any respect. The blue-inexperienced or violet oil-like tarnish, dirt, minerals, or some silver cash' residue have more potent their appearance and need to be left on my own. Dark silver cash need to be wiped clean with ammonia, rubbing alcohol, vinegar, or polish remover with acetone. Do no longer rub or polish them.

Copper Coins – smooth them and soak them in grape oil. If no longer available, olive oil will do. Never attempt to rub them in any manner. However, getting effects may take numerous weeks to a year, so be patient.

Nickel Coins – fantastic wiped smooth with warmth, soapy distilled water using a gentle toothbrush. If cleansing badly stained nickel coins, use ammonia diluted 3 to at the least one with distilled water.

How to Store Your Coins

It might also assist if you stored your coins nicely to keep away from giving them any scratch to lessen their numismatic price. You want to apply the right shape of holder counting on the price of the coin you're storing.

There are folders and albums available commercially that you should buy for storing your series or type series. When the use of paper envelopes, make certain that their materials are specifically best for holding cash, particularly the immoderate-charge ones, at the same time as you hold in thoughts that sulfur or unique chemical materials present in the paper can motive a reaction and alternate the coin's colour.

Plastic flips made from Mylar and acetate are suitable materials for long-time period storage, however thinking about the fact that they'll be hard and brittle, they will scratch the coin if the coins are not inserted and eliminated carefully. "Soft" flips turned into as soon as crafted from polyvinyl chloride (P.V.C.), which decomposed over the years and gave disastrous outcomes for the cash. P.V.C. Lent a green appearance on the coins. P.V.C. Flips aren't produced and acquired inside the U.S.

Tubes can maintain severa equal-length coins and are appropriate for bulk garage of circulated and higher-grade coins if they may be no longer moved. For extra valuable cash, use hard plastic holders as they do no longer incorporate harmful substances and might protect coins towards scratches and wonderful physical damage.

Collectible Coins in their Cases.

You can favor to use slabs for delivered treasured coins as they provide proper safety. Slabs are hermetically sealed hard plastic holders for individual cash. One downside, but, is the price worried

, and you can't be capable of get at the coin without problems if there can be a want to perform that.

Chapter 16: Condition And Characteristics Of The Planchet (Luster Or Brilliance)

Luster is critical in putting in place the truth of a coin is uncirculated or now not. A mint u . S . A . Coin want to be free of placed on and must now not very own any essential harm in its luster. A circulated coin will seem a greater quantity of breaks within the luster and, therefore, show a smaller amount of luster.

Amount and type of put on, harm, and the overall eye attraction of the coin.

The fullness of the strike and luster of a coin shape an frequent satisfactory that is known as "eye enchantment." A coin may be defined as having an incredible eye appeal due to the reality it is sturdy in a single location however may be absolutely suitable in some specific. A coin can be awful in a unmarried region but applicable in some other and may still be referred to as having underneath-commonplace eye appeal. Although eye attraction is subjective, most coin collectors will agree that a positive coin has ideal or terrible eye attraction.

If you want to be a very good coin collector, you need to understand this ability. You can expand this skills thru interplay with awesome professional lenders, reliable and sincere dealers and consulting grading courses. And as with any skill, loads of exercise will provide you with possibilities to enhance. Having a exceptional eye will help loads too.

Grading a coin is considered an art work. It is meant to remember the objective and subjective views that a coin professional has at the same time as analyzing a particular coin. One can objectively determine whether or not or now not or not a coin has been worn or no longer, however how an lousy lot or to what quantity it has affected the coin's not unusual scenario is more difficult to decide.

Not all experts will follow a single assessment - that a coin's floor is of such kingdom, or the nice of the luster is this high, or the fullness of the strike is that this top notch. Added to the mixture is how the ones elements have an effect on and engage. A coin may additionally get preserve of a grade pronouncing it has "extremely good eye enchantment" or some other "excellent eye attraction." In not unusual utilization, superb won't be interchangeable, but its shade of that means is barely indistinguishable from each one-of-a-kind. This may be unique while done to coin grading?

Grading has a set latest. Coin conditions range from the poorest country to the nice united states. A coin in terrible scenario could have neither the date nor designs discernible, even as a coin within the high-quality nation bears designs which might be clean and precise as if they had been just caught on the mint.

However, considering experts are prone to subjectivity, there are various grades that might be assigned to a coin, counting on how the professional views it. Thus, any coin can receive as many grades because the professionals who tested it. This might no longer undermine the expert's opinion, even though. It genuinely indicates how certainly certainly one of a type humans can respect a coin.

Being capable of form your personal assessment of a coin's grade then is essential. As the primary talent in coin collection, you have so as to determine whether or now not or no longer a coin is mint usa; that is, it has no seen signs and symptoms of damage on any of its surface; or circulated, because of this it bears marks of floor placed on because of managing.

Before the Nineteen Forties, the use of adjectives have become the pleasant way to give an explanation for a coin's grade. The numerical grading device in current use became invented via Dr. William Sheldon in that decade. The circulated coin grades have been assigned numbers from 1 to fifty nine, while numbers 60 to 70 have been used for the mint kingdom coins. Zero is the least applicable, and 70 is a coin in a first-rate usa of the united states. This big, but, is applicable to U.S. Coins first-class. An abbreviation for an adjective is appended to the big range for readability.

Using adjectives to grade cash changed into a very subjective and tough device because of the fact a V.F. For one professional can be an E.F. For every other. In truth, coin dealers have regularly been accused of over-grading a coin that permits you to get a better price for his or her products. The addition of the relative numerical precision of the Sheldon scale has helped to make a standardized adjectival grading.

Sheldon's numerical machine is now used by maximum coin collectors and dealers. The

following are based on the Official A.N.A.
Grading Standards for United States Coin:

aG-three

 About Good

G-four

 Good

VG-8

 Very Good

VG-10

 Very Good Plus

F-12

 Fine

F-15

 Fine Plus

VF-20

 Very Fine

Chapter 17: Presidential Coins Proof Set

Grading of proofs is just like the grades used for uncirculated coins using PR 60 to PR 70. PR 70 is unusual or nonexistent if a few instances. A evidence coin may be mishandled or show placed on due to cleaning. This truth can decrease the grade of the coin below PR 60. Proof cash can show tarnishing or darkening too, just like uncirculated cash.

D. Split Grades.

A break up grade is given to a coin while massive versions exist the various obverse and the reverse elements. This grade is denoted with a "/".Normally, the coin's general grade is determined through its worst element. Again, an intermediate fee can be given while the distinction is massive, mainly if the alternative is decrease. For instance, a coin with a grade of MS 60/61 might possibly have an ordinary grade of MS 60, and a few other coin with MS 65/sixty three might have an usual grade of MS sixty four.

Where Can you Find Coins?

Finding Rare and Collectible Coins

For many human beings, coin collecting began out as a interest. Nonetheless, you could listen one-of-a-type people say (or you have got maximum possibly heard your self) about the information of humans making the maximum of their antique cash. This added on more humans to embark on a coin-gathering spree. If you want to begin collecting coins, there are numerous places to start.